LITTLE CHILDREN BLOW YOUR TRUMPETS

THE FAMILY HISTORY *of* ALICE FRAZIER BOULDIN

By Patricia Washington

Please direct all correspondence and book orders to:
Patricia Washington
email: danlni@yahoo.com

Library of Congress Control Number 2010920362
ISBN 978-0-615-34317-4

Published for the author by
Otter Bay Books
3507 Newland Road
Baltimore, MD 21218

www.Otter-Bay-Books.com

Printed in the United States of America

To

ALYCE
TANYA, CHARLES,
&
DANIELLE

The New Day

FROM A VISION RED WITH WAR I AWOKE
AND SAW THE PRINCE OF PEACE
HOVERING OVER NO MAN'S LAND.

LOUD THE WHISTLES BLEW AND THE THUNDER OF CANNON
WAS DROWNED BY THE HAPPY SHOUTING OF THE PEOPLE.

FROM THE SINAI THAT FACES ARMAGEDDON
I HEARD THIS CHANT
FROM THE THROATS OF WHITE-ROBED ANGELS:

BLOW YOUR TRUMPETS, LITTLE CHILDREN!
FROM THE EAST AND FROM THE WEST,
FROM THE CITIES IN THE VALLEY,
FROM GOD'S DWELLING ON THE MOUNTAIN,
BLOW YOUR BLAST THAT PEACE MIGHT KNOW
SHE IS QUEEN OF GOD'S GREAT ARMY.

Fenton Johnson
1888-1958

TABLE *of* CONTENTS...

ALICE AND UNIDENTIFIED WOMAN POSE IN SERVANT'S
UNIFORMS. CIRCA 1890, BROOKLYN, NEW YORK.

ACKNOWLEDGMENTS

A special thank you to my cousin Alyce Baker for her many blessings. Thank you for believing in me. What an honor you have bestowed upon me, without your support this book would not have been possible. To the fifth grade students of Simpson Waverly Elementary-2005-2006, and your wonderful teachers Mrs. Young, and Ms. Oliver, your love of history, primary documents, and research has been an inspiration to me. To Mrs. Adelaide Dixon Hall, I was delighted to meet you. You told me that I spoke with my hand's the same way you remembered Alice Frazier Bouldin, I took your words and placed them in my heart, what a gift they were. To have met someone who knew my great grandmother was a humbling experience for both my family and I. To Mr. Bernard Brown for your help at Fairview Cemetery, not only did we find my great grandmother, but other ancestors who we thought were lost to time. What if you had not offered to look through that ledger one last time, or go out on your own to see if there were any stones buried underground, we would not have found Charles or Milly? I am grateful to the Maryland School for The Deaf and the Frederick Historical Society for their patience in assisting me with my research. My sincere gratitude to the owner's of the Coale-Sappington House, and the Tyler-Page home. To my very dear friends, Winette, Tee, Kim, Reggie, Georgette, and Katrina thank you for taking this journey with me.

Acknowledgement is made to the following for permission to reprint previously published material:

1.　**The Maryland School For The Deaf:** 1938 Maryland Bulletin article on William Downs and Alice Frazier Bouldin. Photo of Old Main Building, Lines from daily log dated April 1929, May 1929, June 1929 regarding William Downs.

2.　*The Frederick News Post:* Obituary for Laura Frazier Downs, "The Work of Death". June 1914. Obituary of Peter Frazier March 1886. "Lincoln Topic before Club" February 1957.

3.　**The Frederick Historical Society:** Page from the 1859 Frederick City Directory, "F". Excerpt from the Maryland Genealogical Resource Guide pp. 269 baptismal records of Frazier children. Copy of Alice Frazier Bouldin's 1934 Affidavit. Excerpt from Frederick Examiner 1853- pp. 12, obituary of Susan Tyler Peck, and Medical Examiners report for 1853 pp. 16. Copy of 1887 map of Klineharts Alley formerly known as Public Alley. The History of Libertytown pp.13, 2 lines. From the William O Lee Jr. Collection: photo copy of Old Hill Church, Asbury Church 1919 Anniversary Bulletin, photo of "Chairman of Auxiliaries" committee members copied from the Asbury Church 1919 Anniversary Bulletin, 2 lines from the Fredericktonian Lodge No.12 135th Anniversary Bulletin referencing past masters.

Arte
4.　**The Burr Katz Library,** Frederick, Maryland, The Maryland Room: Two pages of the 1800 Libertytown Census records.

5.　**Ancestry.com:** One page each of the Frederick, Maryland census records for the years: 1850, 1860, 1870, and 1880. Copy of draft card for Thomas Williams 1900, one page.

6.　**Maryland State Archives in Annapolis:** Fragment of Frederick, Maryland Marriage Log "O" 1872. Slave Assessment Record for District 1 Frederick, Maryland 1852, two pages. Chancery Court Papers 1790 John Young vs. Richard Coale 1797, six lines. Nine pages taken from land records for Frederick, Maryland: Sale of Peter Frazier two pages 1826, deeds for Public Alley, 1853, 1874, 1884, 1903, four pages. Copy of Richard Coale manumissions three pages.

WITH THE CRYING BLOOD OF MILLIONS
WE HAVE WRITTEN DEEP HER NAME
IN THE BOOK OF ALL THE AGES;
WITH THE LILIES IN THE VALLEY,
WITH THE ROSES BY THE MERSEY,
WITH THE GOLDEN FLOWER OF JERSEY
WE HAVE CROWNED HER SMOOTH YOUNG TEMPLES.
WHERE HER FOOTSTEPS CEASE TO FALTER
GOLDEN GRAIN WILL GREET THE MORNING,
WHERE HER CHARIOT DESCENDS
SHALL BE BROKEN DOWN THE ALTARS
OF THE GODS OF DARK DISTURBANCE.

Fenton Johnson
1888-1958

INTRODUCTION

Pike's Daughter

My father Pike was born Charles Lewis Bouldin on April 15, 1910 in Hudson, New York. He was the firstborn son of Charles William and Sara Fanny Bouldin. My father met my mother Diana Washington sometime during the early 1960's and by 1965 they had four children, Charles, Tanya, Patricia, and Terrance. Though we were raised primarily by our mother we spent many weekends and summers with Pike. When I was eight years old and my sister Tanya nine, we began to see our father on our own, as we grew older I would often visit alone, my other siblings chose not to go as often as I, or not at all. Those were great times-that I spent with my father, who was by the time I was ten in his early sixties. My father was tall, and very strong. He was an intelligent, adventurous, and whimsical man, who commandeered the attention of everyone in his presence. For most of his life he was a long distance trucker, eventually settling down in his retirement age in the state of Maine, a place he often travelled to in his work.

During the late 1960's many of the families in my South Bronx neighborhood maintained strong family ties in the southern states. Families now living in the north had been part of the "Great Migration", the movement of blacks from the rural south to cities in the north. One particular summer when I was about nine years old I recall that many of my friends were either going down south for the summer to stay with family, or had cousins from the south who were staying with them. This exchange sparked my curiosity, and I decided to ask my own mother why we could not do the same. I remember thinking that there must be someone who we could visit, or who could visit us, but I soon found out that there was no one. According to my mother the only family we had was in New York City. She told me that her father Clarence Washington had been adopted and as far as she knew he was born in New York. Today I know that my maternal great grandmother, Margaret Hill was born and raised in Charlotte, North Carolina. I do not know when or why she left her family in Charlotte, but in 1920 my maternal grandmother Lois Washington was born in Harlem, New York.

My mother was the eldest of five siblings. Growing up we were a small close knit family. For years we did everything together, cookouts, birthdays, holidays, and graduations. It was a beautiful thing, being raised so close, spending time with my grandmother, aunt, uncles, and cousins. Nevertheless, my young mind could not believe that was it, what happened to all of the ancestors I had read about in the library? Surely there were other family members somewhere, how could there be no line to follow? To me it was as simple as plotting a straight line from my parents to their parents, and so it bothered me greatly to think that my story extended only as far as my eyes could see. And though I never bothered my mother again about her family, I vowed to learn all that I could about Pike's.

When I was eleven Pike moved out of state, and I would not see or speak with him again until the death of my mother in 1981. We stayed in touch until his death in 1990, but never at any time did I ask about his family, I really cannot say why, but I like to think now, that it was not the right time.

Just before I went away to college I was introduced to a first cousin, Valera "Libby" Bouldin. Libby was the youngest daughter of Harold, one of Pike's two younger brothers. I spent a lot of time talking with Libby, and though she could tell me many stories about my father and mother, she could tell me very little about the rest of the Bouldin family. Once during one of our conversations she showed me a bible she said belonged to her sister. On one of the family pages in the bible her sister had written the name of our grandfather, Charles William Bouldin. Underneath his name were his birth date, and place of birth, Frederick, Maryland. Though I had attended his funeral in 1972 I knew little else about him, this information had come as a surprise to me, and I was very excited. Today, I can still close my eyes and see Libby's hands at the edge of the page, and the exact placement of the writing. It was a gift, a place to start, somewhere south just below the Mason Dixon line there was a story waiting for me.

I copied down my grandfather's information, swearing that I would ask my father about Frederick, the next time we got together, but I never did. Sometime shortly thereafter I obtained a copy of the 1880 census record for Frederick, Maryland. Written on the census were my grandfather Charles at the age of two, his mother Alice Frazier Bouldin age 25, and father George William Bouldin age 30. For several months after I would look at the census record and envision a lady I believed was Alice wearing a style of dress popular during the late nineteenth century. In the vision she appeared tall and slim-and was always standing in a cemetery. At the time I could not figure out why I kept thinking of her or her name because she was not the one I had set out to follow, I was following the Bouldin name and had already arranged my thoughts around finding George.

In 1987 while living overseas my sister Tanya wrote to say she had attended the funeral of my father's brother Uncle Harold. She told me that all of our father's family was there, and that I had missed an occasion. She mentioned that an Aunt Ida, my father's younger sister had telephoned her after the funeral to document our information for the family tree. Unfortunately any excitement felt by me was to be short lived, because my sister ended her letter by telling me she believed she had lost Aunt Ida's number and had no way of contacting her again. At the time I was disappointed and could not believe my misfortune, but today in hindsight I wonder if the ancestors were working in their way, at their own pace. I can now admit that had I spoken with my Aunt Ida I would have been so overjoyed at meeting her, my search would have come to an end. So my sister Tanya in her own way, helped to tell the story of our family.

Years went by and I would think about them, the Frazier's and Bouldin's. At least twice a year I would post queries on genealogy websites in search of my father's family. I joined the New York City Chapter of African American Genealogy, attended monthly meetings, and shared stories with other would be genealogist. Each month I looked forward to reading their monthly bulletin in hopes that my family's information might be contained in its pages. I even tried searching the telephone directories for each borough in New York City thinking a Bouldin would be listed. Nothing came of these halfhearted inquiries, though my search required commitment and rigor I continued to put a minute into an hour's work believing I would stumble upon something eventually.

In 2003 after a trip to Charlotte to see my sister, I decided to stop by my cousin Harold's home, Harold was Libby's only brother. Ten minutes into my visit with Harold he asked if I had gone to the house on Bushwick Avenue. When I told him I had not, he assured me that there was someone there waiting for me, and wrote down the house number. This was the house my grandfather, several aunts, and uncles lived in from the late nineteen fifties after moving out of Harlem. I knew this house, remembered the tree lined street it was on, and its location on Bushwick Avenue. I knew in my heart that I needed to go see who if anyone still lived in that house, but wasn't sure where I would find the courage to take this next step. Having the house number changed everything it was a precious jewel in my hand. When finally I made the call I was disheartened to learn that my Aunt Ida was the only one left of my father's siblings. To my dismay Aunt Ida had Alzheimer's disease and would not be able to communicate with me. However her daughter Alyce was also living in the home, caring for her ailing mother. Alyce, and I spoke over the telephone for months. She would tell me wonderful stories about our grandfather, my father, aunts, uncles and cousins. I was mesmerized by the love that came from those stories, and wanted to learn more.

Finally after months of talking on the telephone we decided I should visit. Alyce tells me the minute she saw me she knew who I was. She likes to tell me that I look just like Pike, and I agree. As we talked about family, Alyce began to share with me the many photographs that our aunts and uncles had taken over the years. By the time I had left her home that first day I tried to convince myself that I had found what I was searching for, but the picture of Alice Frazier Bouldin in the cemetery hung on the fringes of my mind and I could not ignore it. In June 2004 my Aunt Ida passed away, and Alyce, going through her mother's papers came upon many more photos and documents including a family tree Aunt Ida had begun, the same one that she called my sister about years before.

As we looked through the photos and documents we noticed that there were many related to Alice Frazier Bouldin and her family, the Frazier's. There were no photos of George Bouldin or any other Bouldin except Charles, his wife and children. It was after looking through those papers that I knew I must go to Frederick. On my trip back home I begun to think about Alice Frazier Bouldin standing in that cemetery and it occurred to me that maybe she was trying to guide me to her from the very start. It was at that point I understood why it took so long for me to arrive here. I realized that I could have found the house on my own many years before, that I also could have asked my father about his family. I knew that had I learned of those items years ago I would not have wanted them, and if I had taken them they probably would not exist today. I do not believe that finding my father's family at that moment in time was a coincidence. I believe that the place where I found myself was set in motion many years before when a little girl asked her mother why she did not have any family to visit.

Alice Frazier Bouldin my great grandmother was born into slavery, Alice Frazier on October 27, 1855 in Frederick, Maryland. She was the 10th and last child of Charles and Milly Frazier. By the time of her death in June 1938, Alice had saved many documents and photos about her life, and that of her parents and siblings. These photo's and personal letters were then passed on to her only son, my grandfather Charles William Bouldin. Charles and Sara Fanny Bouldin had nine children, and together they all added to the legacy begun by the Frazier's in Frederick, that is of love and family. Using Alice as my guiding light I was able to fill in some of the missing pieces that now make up this book, a book about the love of family through slavery to the present.

PROLOGUE

Alice's Story

ESTER GAVE HER STORY TO PETER AND CHARLES,

CHARLES SHARED THIS STORY WITH MILLY
AND THEY CREATED ONE OF THEIR OWN,

ALICE GOT IT LAST
AND REMEMBERED IT TO HER CHARLES
WHO SHARED IT WITH SARA FANNY

TOGETHER THEY TOLD A 3RD STORY
TO GO WITH THE TWO BEFORE.

NOW MANY YEARS HAVING PASSED
AND THE STORIES LOST OR FORGOTTEN
AROSE WITH THE FERVOR
OF A TRUMPHET PLAYING LITTLE GIRL,

WHO AWOKE THE ANCESTORS TO PROCLAIM,
THEIR STORY.

LIBERTYTOWN, MARYLAND
RICHARD COALE PLANTATION

February 12, 1812. She marveled at the numbers, even though she had no idea what a twelve looked like, she imagined it to be tall and strong like her. The exactness of it all fascinated her, this was something that she had not even known about herself, or her firstborn Peter, a day of birth, the day her Charles was born. This gift, she thought was enough to set her dreams right for months and she could not move her mind pass it the length of the day.

NINE DAYS EARLIER

When it seemed she was about to burst, because her belly had grown so full she dreamt her baby sound and whole. That next morning she awoke before the cold could loosen its grip on the sun. When she arrived at the main house Ester tried to erase any sounds or thoughts of numbers that were in her head. The ones that were hiding in the corners, (like the number of times she had awakened last night); were the hardest to erase but she focused her thoughts. She did not want any other number in her head besides the number of the day she knew she would soon find out. Ester could not write it down because she had not known how to shape numbers or letters to make words, besides she had no writing tool. No, this time she would remember and count up every day that passed until she gave birth. So she kept it, the number Jinny the head cook had supplied her with that cold winter morning, right in the front of her head. From that day Ester began the count until finally without having to start with a new moon, her second boy was born, and his birth date was February 12, 1812.

One morning when Peter was six and Charles five Ester awoke from the most glorious of dreams. She dreamt of Peter and Charles floating high above her in the sky, with wings instead of arms, were they birds or angels? She could not tell which, but she knew that they were free. It was then that Ester began to sing to her two sons. At first it began with a few words she had harmonized into song as they fell asleep. Soon her songs turned into stories that she made them promise never to share with a soul. Each night she would tell them the story of Peter and Charles, and how they became free as men, and cared for one another and their families. She would tell them of their strength, and kindness, and respect for God and the land. Oh, Ester was full of stories, surprising even herself, for she had never known freedom, and knew of no one else who had either. Even so, none of that had mattered to Ester, and she continued her made up stories right into their teen years. From the start Ester would always tell a part of the story where they might be taken away from each other or from her. This part always made Charles cry out in protest, but Ester would Sshh! him with her eyes and continue on. As painful as it was even Ester knew that she was doing the right thing by telling them the truth. She'd been witness too many times to recall, and though she could not remember her own separation she knew that someplace in time a family still mourned for her. Ester prayed nightly for it not to happen to her, but the chunk of ice that had formed in the space between her breasts never seemed to melt. In fact it seemed to grow larger and colder each time she had given birth. Isham was the strongest man she had ever seen or known, black or white, and he was brave too. They were never married, not in the way the white folks were, and they were never allowed to live together either. Isham was a hire-out slave. His expertise as a blacksmith, allowed Master Coale to hire him out to work on contract to whoever could pay. Sometimes Isham was gone for only a week or so, but lately he had been gone for months at a time, and like with Peter, Isham did not see Charles until he was almost walking.

For a while things had been good, and Isham had stayed put. When Briel was born Isham had been right by her side, but that was short-lived. It seemed like whenever they were having children Isham was sent away. Right after baby girl's birth he was hired out to some wealthy people in Georgia. Weeks and months passed but he did not return, ever, and nobody thought her and their three children enough to be told.

DECEMBER 1826

All morning long Ester knew something was coming, her baby girl who she had tied to her hip cried all morning long. Ester tried everything to comfort her, extra feedings, her favorite song, but nothing worked. She had worked straight through the noon zenith washing three full tubs of clothes, then hanging each garment on the tree line for drying out. She was exhausted, and had not planned on working straight through, but Briel's agitation motivated her to finish most of her work quickly. Just as this thought was clearing her mind she looked up to see Charles running full speed through the fields waving his arms and yelling something she could not quite make out. Her heart began to fill, Isham had come back to them. Ester quickly rose from her kneeling position, gathering Briel, and moving at a fast pace to greet Charles. She was all nerves, happy, and jittery, trying to fix her hair, shifting baby girl from one hip to the other so that Isham could see her good side. She was so immersed in her own thoughts that it was not until Charles stood within an arm's reach that she heard his words. Ester knew what the matter was, oh she knew for sure, and Briel had known it too, and had tried to tell her all morning long. She grabbed her youngest son by the elbow and Sshhed! him with her eyes. Her heart was leaping around furiously and the skin on her bones was pouring sweat out of every pore it owned. After allowing the respectful time to pass for a child when he has been told to be quiet, Charles told his mother that Peter was gone. Master Coale had sold Peter. Ester stood erect now and gazed at her son. She wanted to speak, to cry, to scream, but nothing left her mouth not even air. She was drowning, the ice between her breasts had begun to melt filling her chest and lungs. Ester could not breathe now even if she wanted to. She could barely stand, the sudden rush of water had made her body feel all wobbly. The water, now warm, had taken control, flooding her body parts, she was a million tears. Ester would not allow a teardrop to fall, if she did she knew they would all fall and she would be gone to herself and her two remaining children forever. Somehow she managed to freeze them, but not before thinking that this awful place she was in was death, she had died.

Ester pushed her second son aside and headed toward the main house. They must have known she'd come, because Master Coale was standing right out in front. Ester knew what he was going to say, she had heard him tell the same to others, but what explaining could you do to someone whose world you have just removed from beneath their feet.

After Ester heard all that she could bear she turned her body so that she was facing Charles and staring right into his eyes. "I don't care about a sell," she said. "I'm telling you, that you will see your brother, you will visit your brother". Charles was taken aback by his mother's stern, almost threatening tone. She had warned them of this day, the day when one of them might be sold away, from her or each other. She had told them both almost every night since they were little.

Charles closed his eyes for a moment to hear her words, "Peter, Charles, one day they are going to take you away from me, they are not going to ask me or tell me they are just going to do it. So you two have to be clear in your minds, that I may not see you again. When you do, it will be alright because I tied your hearts to each other in such a way that no man can undo."

"I DID THESE THINGS
WHEN YOU HAD LITTLE FEET,
BECAUSE I KNEW THIS DAY WOULD COME."

Nevermore shall men know suffering,
Nevermore shall women wailing
Shake to grief the God of Heaven.

From the East and from the West,
From the cities in the valley,

From God's dwelling on the mountain,
Little children,
blow your trumpets!

Fenton Johnson
1888-1958

CHAPTER 1

Ester

$\mathcal{S}$ometime during the late 18th century a child was born, and she was named Ester. The details of Ester's birth are unknown as are the identities of her parents, siblings, or the father of her two sons, Peter and Charles. Frederick, Maryland census records from 1850 through 1880 show that both Peter and Charles state their parents were born in Maryland. If this information is correct then the removal of the Frazier's from their ancestral land of Africa did not occur within Ester's generation. Ester lived in Libertytown, Maryland, a small town located in the eastern part of Frederick County. The existence of Ester and her relation to Libertytown comes by way of a manumission paper belonging to her son Charles who was the property of Richard Coale, owner of Libertytown.

In 1754 John Young purchased Duke Woods from the Arnold Livers Estate. By 1782 he renamed it Libertytown, divided it into parts and began selling tracts of land for sale or rent. During this same time John Young began a relationship with Richard Coale, a businessman who had interest in mining. In 1783 Richard Coale built his home called the Coale Mansion at the center of town, at the time it was the largest in Libertytown. However much the two regarded each other as friends, business dealings were quite another matter. In an affidavit filed by John Young in 1797 against his friend Richard Coale, John Young accused Richard Coale of reneging on a contract to lease several Negro slaves. In his complaint John Young claimed that Richard Coale was intending to injure and defraud him. In his defense Richard Coale stated that Young disposed of all his land, had no plantation in which to work his Negroes and agreed to let him have the use of them until the terms of a sale was made. This did little to ruin the friendship, in fact when John Young died, having no relatives he willed all of Libertytown to Richard Coale whose wealth was increased. Of course John Young and Richard Coale were not the only slave owners in Libertytown, according to Scharf's History of Western Maryland, during the Revolutionary War conflict and for some time after, the Libertytown area was the largest slave holding district of the county. In the 1800 census record for Libertytown Richard Coale owned 30 slaves, in the same census record there was a Thomas Frazier Sr. who owned 26 slaves. The total count for slaves in the Libertytown district was 1176. Subsequently a search of land records for Frederick County for the years 1748 through 1834, show specific transactions relating to the sale, purchase, and release of slaves, these transactions were found in deeds, mortgages, repossessions, manumissions, and other sales.

It is quite probable that Ester was owned by either Thomas Frazier or John Young prior to becoming the property of Richard Coale. Whoever owned Ester she was likely to have been one of the 1176 slaves recorded in the census numbers for Libertytown in 1800.

A search of manumissions originating from Richard Coale showed that he often listed the names and relationships of persons he was setting free. This may or may not have been unique to Richard Coale. Whether he was just keeping track of his property, or repenting the iniquities of slavery one can only guess at.

No documents have been found that suggest Ester's freedom, the status of her two sons imply she remained a slave throughout her natural life, and no liberty was ever given to her. As I write I try to envision Ester, and find that there is no space in my mind to fit what Ester may have seen and felt in her lifetime.

By the year 1847 both of Ester's sons, Peter and Charles were liberated from slavery. Peter, his wife and children were all free by the year 1850, but Charles though free would remain in bondage through his wife and children. This bulwark of slavery guaranteed the continued degradation of his wife and children who remained enslaved, and the disparagement of Charles who was free.

Charles Frazier's wife and children were owned by Dr. William Tyler, the grandfather of William Tyler Page, author of The American Creed. Dr. William Tyler came to Frederick in the late 1790's and studied medicine under his brother John Tyler. In 1811 William Tyler was elected to the Maryland House of Delegates for Frederick County, he was a chairman, a committeeman, a secretary for the Republican Party, and a good friend of President Jackson. In 1817 he was elected president of the Farmers and Mechanics National Bank of Frederick, a position he held for 55 years. Dr. William Tyler had two sons and three daughters, William, Samuel, Eleanor, Susan, and Christiana. In the 1850 census for free inhabitants in the Tyler household, listed after his wife and five children is

RICHARD COALE
1760-1834.

the name of a free man employed as a laborer, Charles Frazier. Two years later in a Frederick County Slave Assessment for District Number 1 appears Dr. William Tyler again, this time; his slaves are listed and valued: Charles age seven: seventy-five dollars, Lewis age five: seventy-five dollars, Laura age one: fifty dollars and Milly age forty-one: one hundred dollars. According to the assessment record Dr. William Tyler owned 4 slaves, they were called Negroes then, and in 1852, they were from one family, Alice Frazier Bouldin's family.

Frederick County, Maryland, 1800 Census - Liberty Town District #7												
Head of the family	Free white males					Free white females					Other free persons	Number of slaves
	Under 10	10 - 16	16 - 26	26 - 45	Over 45	Under 10	10 - 16	16 - 26	26 - 45	Over 45		
Champer, Jacob	4	1			1		1		1			
Chaney, Charles		1			1	3	1		1			
Chaney, Sophia	2								1			
Charby, George				1					1			
Charlton, John W.	1				1	5			1			6
Chinwalt, Thomas	1	1		1	1	2	2	4		1		
Clapsadle, Paul		1	2		1	1	1	2		1		
Clark, Josia	2	3	1	1		1			1			
Clark, Seth				1		2			1		1	
Clark, William	3		1	1			1	1	1			
Clary, Benjamin		1	3	1	1		2	1	1			
Clary, Daniel	1		1	1		4			1			1
Clary, David	3	1	1	1		1	1	1	1			
Clary, Rachel		2	1			3	1			1		
Clay, John	3		1	1		1			1			
Climsen, John	2	1	2	1		1	1	1	1			1
Cniser, Michael	2	1		1		2			1			
Coale, Richard	1			1		4	1		1			30
Cockran, Elizabeth		1	1			1				1		
Coke, Adam	2	2		1		3			1			
Colliburg, Frederick	2			1			2	1	1			
Colliburger, John	1			1		3			1			
Collins, Reese			1			1		1				
Comston, Joshua			1			1		1		1		
Condal, David			1		1			1		1		
Condal, Zacharia	2			1				1		1		
Condel, David Junr	1			1				1				
Connel, David	1			1				1				
Cook, Casper	1	2	1	1		2				1		
Cook, Elizabeth										1		5
Cookerly, Jacob	4	1		1		3			1		1	2
Cookerly, John		2	1		1					1		3
Cooms, Henry		1			1		1			1		
Coonse, Mary			1				1		1			
Corry, James	3			1		1			1			
Covil, Jonathan	3	2			1		1	2	2			
Cox, Joshua	1			1	1	2			1	1		1
Cox, Samuel		1			1		1		1			9
Coyle, Joseph				1		1		1				
Crabb, John					1	4			1			1
Crapster, Abraham			1	1					1			2
Crawford, Jonas		1		1	1			1		1		
Crawford, Mathias	3			1		1	1		1			
Creager, Adam	1	1	2	2	1	3	1	1	2	1		1
Creager, Conrod		1		1	1	1		1		1		4
Creager, Henry	3		2	1	1	1	1			1		
Creager, Henry of Conrod	1	1	2	1		2		1				1
Creamer, Adam	2		1	1				1	1			
Creamer, Catherine										1		
Creamer, George	1			1		1		1				

1800 Census Record for Libertytown, Maryland. Richard Coale owned many tracts of farmland in Libertytown. An owner who held thirty slaves-beyond having some wealth would have had to have land in which to work this number of slaves, or a large home that required such a number.

Frederick County, Maryland, 1800 Census - Election District #3

Head of the family	Free white males					Free white females					Other free persons	Number of slaves
	Under 10	10 - 16	16 - 26	26 - 45	Over 45	Under 10	10 - 16	16 - 26	26 - 45	Over 45		
Fister, Henry	2			1				1				
Fister, Jacob	1	1		1				1	1			
Flight, John			1	1		2		1				1
Flook, Jacob	2			1		2			1			
Fluck, Barbara								1		1		
Fluck, John	2	1			1	3	1		1			
Fluck, Mathias	2	1		1		2	1	1	1			
Forest, Jacob	1	2	1		1	1		1	1			
Forrest, Jonathan	1	1			1	1	1		1	1		
Fortney, David	2		2			1		1				
Fortney, Peter	2		1					1				
Fox, Frederick		1	2		1		1	3	1			
Frazier, Jonathan	2	1	1		1	3	3		1			8
Frazier, Levy			1			1		1				
Frazier, Rebecca		1	2					1	1			
Frazier, Sarah			1					4		1		1
Frazier, Thomas Senr				1					1			26
Frazier, William	3	2	1	1		1		1				2
Frazzer, John			1									
Frazzer, John S.	3			1								
Frine, Susanna			1							1		
Fry, Isaac		1	1			1		1				
Fry, John			1					1				
Fry, Jonathan		1		1				2		1		
Fryberger, George	2			1		1	1	1				1
Fulten, George	1			1		1		1				1
Funk, Rudolph	2		1		1	2	2		1			
Gaber, Peter			1		1		1	1	1	1		
Gaber, Samuel	3		1	1		1			1			
Garret, Barton			1		1	1		3		1		14
Garret, Eanos			1					1				9
Garret, John D.			3					1				10
Garret, John M.	2		1	1		1			1		1	5
Garret, John P.		2										1
Garret, Joseph			1					1				3
Gay, Henry	2	1			1		1	2		1		
Gebhart, Jacob	2				1	1	1		1			
Geisinger, Charles	2	1			1	2				1		
Gelaspie, Mathew	2				1	2	1	1	1			
Germnant, George	1	1	1		1	3	2		1			
Getz, Jacob		1			1				1			
Getzenger, Martin	2			1		2			1			
Giddings, Colmore	2			1		2			1			15
Giddings, Erasmus			1					1				4
Giddings, Jane		1	1				1	1		1		18
Gilbert, Christian	1	1			1	1	1	1		1		
Gilbert, Jeremiah	4	1		1		1	1		1			
Glover, Samuel	1			1				1				
Goodman, Christian				1							1	

1800 Census Record. Thomas Frazier, Sr. owned 26 slaves. To further the institution of slavery Africans names were replaced with Christian names. These surnames remain with us today, a haunting memory of slavery and its practices. While some blacks had one owner throughout slavery, others had many. Sometimes they took on the name of the new owner, and other times chose to keep the name of their first owner, still others when freedom came chose an altogether different name.

Coale-Sappington House located in Libertytown, Maryland built in 1783 by Richard Coale. In 2007 the current owner of the home was gracious enough to allow me to see the inside of the home, which has changed little since its construction. On the left side-view of the home on the first floor are two small windows and a large one. These are the kitchen and pantry. On the second floor of the same view are three small windows and a larger one, the larger of the second floor windows were the slave quarters. The design of the slave quarters was such that it could be accessed from the kitchen via a stairway which led directly from the room. Once inside the kitchen a door leading outside allowed the slaves to enter the main house through yet another door. This back door was used to bring in items from the kitchen without having to walk through the home. *Photo courtesy of Mrs. Rosemarie Sappington, 2002.*

Tyler home, 109-111 Record Street the Tyler-Page home in Frederick Maryland. In 1843 a fire destroyed the upper floors of the original building, however William Tyler was able to rebuild and replace those areas damaged by the fire. A letter written from a Frederick citizen to her sister who lived out of town noted that it was a very large fire, and no injury or loss of life occurred. Dr. William Tyler owned all of the homes on the block, which were occupied by his children. The home has many fireplaces, and a huge pit oven. During my visit the owners and I tried to figure out where the slave quarters might have been, but it is a large home and no one space stood out. However there is a mother-in-law subdivision with its own entrance and exit. This may have been the slave quarters. At one point it was thought that the Frazier's may have lived in the slave quarters located down the block on Church Street, but this was immediately struck down as Alice in her own words stated that she was born in and lived in the house on Record Street. *Photo, courtesy of Maurice and Diane Daugherty, 2009.*

Copies of Slave Sales, Purchases, and Manumissions
Made by Richard Coale

Copy of manumission found in Land Records for Frederick County. It was not unusual for slaves or freed relatives to purchase themselves if given the opportunity. Here Richard Coale states he received two hundred dollars for the freedom of his slaves Mariah and Harriet.

At the Request of Richard Coale the following deed is recorded September 20th. 1828

To all to whom it may concern be it known that I Richard Coale of Frederick County and state of Maryland for divers good causes and consideration me thereunto making is also in further consideration of two hundred dollars current money to me in hand paid or secured to be paid have released from slavery liberated, manumitted, and set free and by these presents do hereby release from slavery, liberated manumit and set free , my two negro women, Mariah and Harriet daughter of Mary Bryan deceased, the said Mariah being of the age of thirty eight, and the said Harriet of the age of eighteen, both being able to work and gain a sufficient livelihood and maintenance, and them the said negro women named, I do declare to be henceforth free, manumitted and discharged from all manner of servitude or service to me, my executors, or administrators forever.

Enslaved Blacks were considered less than human, and treated as chattel. This document shows that in 1831 Richard Wilson sold his entire estate to Richard Coale, included with the farming and household items are a family of slaves. This person was either moving far away or had fallen upon hard times and needed to raise money.

At the Request of Richard Coale the following sale is recorded 18th April 1831

Know all men by these presents that I Richard Wilson of Frederick County and state of Maryland for and in consideration of the sum of two thousand dollars current money to me in hand paid by Richard Coale of the county and state aforesaid at and before the sealing and delivery hereof the receipt whereof I do hereby acknowledge have granted bargained and sold and by these presents do grant bargain and sell unto the said Richard Coale his executors administrators and afsigns all the following property to wit Henry Blackman and Betty his wife and Dick Westly, Maria, Henry, Abraham, Jacob, William, Kitty and Betty their children. Also Harriet Mulatto woman and Elizabeth her child, three steers, one bull: windmill; seven ploughs; two wagons; cutting box; one sleigh; one grind stove; thirty barrels of corn; forty bushels of Rye; twenty acres of rye in the ground; forty acres of wheat; four mahogany tables; eighteen chairs; one sideboard; five waiters; set of...

7

Manumission by Richard Coale of a dark mulatto slave named Miranda. In this document he identifies Miranda's mother as a free woman named Charity. He also states that Miranda at the age of eighteen is capable of supporting herself. Whatever jobs she may have held as a slave would be counted on to help her find employment. These skills would be vital to Miranda's survival as a free woman. Blacks when freed had many obstacles they had to overcome if they wanted to survive. Besides having a job, they had to have a place to live, and know the laws for free blacks. Though they were no longer slaves, in Frederick there were laws that forbade them to assemble after dark, and one that prevented them from being on the streets after 7:30 p.m. These newly freed slaves also had to be wary of circumstances and people who might have them sold back into slavery. Manumission found in the Land Records for Frederick County.

At the Request of Richard Coale the following manumission is recorded 16th April 1829

To all whom it may concern be it known that I Richard Coale of Frederick County in the state of Maryland for divers good causes and consideration me cherurts? Moving as also in further consideration of one dollar current money to me in hand paid have released from slavery liberated manumitted and set free my dark mulatto woman Miranda daughter of Charity a free negro woman the said Miranda being of the age of eighteen and able to work and gain a sufficient livelihood and maintenance and the said negro woman Idada-slave to be henceforth free manumitted and discharged from all manner of servitude or service to me my executors or administrators forever. In testimony whereof I have hereto set free my hand and affixed my seal this 22nd day of October eighteen hundred and twenty-eight signed sealed and deliver in presence of us John Gliean and William Coale.

8

I do declare

1850 census record for Frederick Maryland. Lines 8-11 are of Peter Frazier, his wife Hannah, daughter Mary Margaret, and son Thomas. Peter and his two children are described as "B" Black, while Hannah has an "M" for Mulatto. Free blacks maintained family ties, and worked to support those families. This record shows seven families including the Frazier's in which the male head of household was employed.

9

FROM ETHIOPIA, GROANING 'NEATH HER HEAVY BURDENS,
I HEARD THE MUSIC OF THE OLD SLAVE SONGS.

I HEARD THE WAIL OF WARRIORS, DUSK BROWN,
WHO GRIMLY FOUGHT THE FIGHT OF OTHERS IN THE TRENCHES OF MARS.

I HEARD THE PLEA OF BLOOD-STAINED MEN OF DUSK
AND THE CRIMSON IN MY VEINS
LEAPT FURIOUSLY.

Fenton Johnson
1888-1958

CHAPTER 2
Peter & Hannah Frazier

Peter Frazier was the brother of Charles. In 1826 at the age of fifteen Peter Frazier was sold by Richard Coale to Eli Umstead of Frederick for the sum of three hundred fifty dollars. Included in the sale were provisions for Peter's freedom, which were to be after twenty years of servitude to Eli Umstead. By 1850 Peter had a wife, Hannah, a mulatto, a daughter Mary Margaret age six and son Thomas age two, and they were all free. A record of Mary Margaret's baptism at All Saints Church in Frederick states that she was born August 28, 1843 and was baptized on December 21st of the same year. Peter was not yet free when Mary Margaret was born, but was, by the birth of his son Thomas. No information has been found to confirm the status of Hannah before 1850. So it is difficult to say when she gained her freedom, whether or not she was born free, or if daughter Mary Margaret had ever been considered a slave. Hannah's story remains a mystery, though there were photos of unknown women found, none could be specifically identified as Hannah, and no other documents have been located. According to the Fairview Cemetery ledger, Hannah Frazier died in 1880. When her husband Peter died in 1886, there was no mention of either Hannah or their two children in his obituary. Both children seem to have vanished. Were they sold into slavery? Did they die early of disease or other injury? Mary Margaret's baptism record noted that she was ill. Whatever the circumstances neither child was found in any census record pass 1870, and when William Downs and Alice Frazier Bouldin passed away surviving relatives were noted but none were Peter and Hannah's children.

Peter and his brother Charles remained in close contact after they were freed. Together in 1853 they obtained a mortgage from the Fredericktown Savings Institution to purchase property on Public Alley in Frederick.

I imagine that Ester prepared her sons for the glaring indignities of slavery as best she could, knowing that each day she looked upon their faces could be her last. In the end a mother's love would be victorious, the brothers bond would not be broken. In November 2006 while searching for the burial place of Alice Frazier Bouldin, it was discovered that Peter and Charles were also in the same block and lot.

Peter Frazier sold at age fifteen.

At the request of Eli Umstead the following sale and manumission are recorded December 28th 1826.
Know all men by these presents that I Richard Coale of Frederick County and state of Maryland for and in consideration of the sum of three hundred and fifty dollars current money to me in hand paid by Eli Umstead of the County and state aforesaid the receipt whereof I do hereby acknowledge and granted bargained and sold and delivered and by this present so grant bargain sell and deliver unto the said Eli Umstead my negro slave named Peter Frashier being at this time about fifteen years of age, which said slave Peter Frashier lives warrants and defend to the said Eli Umstead his executors administrators and afsigns against me my executors administrators
(Continued on next page)

12

(Continued from previous page)

and against any other person or persons whomsoever and be it known that I Richard Coale for divers good causes and consideration me thereunto moving and also for the further sum of five dollars current money to me in hand paid the receipts whereof I do acknowledge and hereby declare the said slave Peter Frashier after he serves the said twenty years as herein before mentioned free manumitted released from slavery liberated and discharged from any manner of servitude or service to me my executors administrators forever, in testimony whereof I have hereunto set my hand and affixed my seal.

December 18th, 1826   Richard Coale
Signed sealed and delivered in the presence of Abm Jones, Abdiet. Abdiel Unkofer

This sale of Peter was located in the Land Records for Frederick County under Richard Coale. The manumission paper that survived for Charles prompted me to review all related court records of Richard and James M. Coale in search of Peter and Ester. Though Ester was not found we now know Peter's fate prior to 1850. As I read through the sale I noticed that the surname Frazier was spelled differently, in the sale it is spelled Frashier. Whether this was an error, or the proper spelling of the name at the time I am unsure. This was a significant find in my research, it allowed me to connect Peter Frazier to Richard Coale, as well as document his age and status before 1850, where he appeared in the census as a free inhabitant of Frederick, Maryland.

Page No. _151_ 70

SCHEDULE 1.—Free Inhabitants in _Frederick City_ in the County of _Frederick_ State of _Maryland_ enumerated by me, on the _22d_ day of _June_ 1860. _Wm H. Laley_ Ass't Marshal.

Post Office _Frederick City_.

Dwelling-houses numbered in the order of visitation.	Families numbered in the order of visitation.	The name of every person whose usual place of abode on the first day of June, 1860, was in this family.	Age.	Sex.	White, black, or mulatto.	Profession, Occupation, or Trade of each person, male and female, over 15 years of age.	Value of Real Estate.	Value of Personal Estate.	Place of Birth, Naming the State, Territory, or Country.	Married within the year.	Attended School within the year.	Persons over 20 y'rs of age who cannot read & write.	Whether deaf and dumb, blind, insane, idiotic, pauper, or convict.
1	2	3	4	5	6	7	8	9	10	11	12	13	14
1158	1145	William Purdy	45	m	B	Laborer	300	Med					
		Margaret d	40	f	B								
		John Johnson	5	m	B								
1159	1146	John Rose	57	m	m	Laborer	350						
		Killis d	42	f	m								
		May d	9	f	m								
		Charles d	6	m	m								
		Ann d	11	f	B								
1160	1147	Peter Frazier	48	m	B	Laborer	300						
		Hannah d	50	f	B								
		Margaret d	17	f	B								
		Thomas d	13	m	B								
		Laura Roles	7	f	B								
		Wm Williams	27	m	m	Laborer							
1161	1148	John Roberson	35	m	B								
		Mary d	19	m	B								
		Kesa d	65	m	B								
1162	1149	William Brown	44	m	B	Laborer							
		Mary d	40	f	B								
		Harriett d	20	f	B								
		Susan d	18	f	B								
		Kesa d	16	f	B								
		Satilla d	14	f	B								
		William d	11	m	B								
		John d	9	m	B								
		Thomas d	8	m	B								
		Frank d	7	m	B								
		Ann d	6	f	B								
		Eliza d	2	f	B								
	1150	William Williams	25	m	m	Brick Maker							
		Susan d	23	f	m								
		Caroline Chaston	50	f	m								
	1151	James Bentley	20	m	m								
		Sarah d	18	f	m								
		Andrew d	10	m	m								
	1152	John Hegler	45	m		Laborer	300	100	Bavaria, Germany				
		Kate d	40	f									
		Anna d	18	f									
	1153	Frank Zeller	44	m		Laborer							
		Odella d	31	f									

No. white males, _9_ No. colored males, _18_ No. foreign born, ____ No. blind, ____

No. deaf and dumb, ____ No. insane, ____

No. idiotic, ____ No. paupers, ____

No. convicts, ____

Often extended family members or other non relatives lived in the households of other free blacks, (lines 3, 13, 14, 32, and 33). Lines 18-29 are of a husband and wife and their ten children, all free and living in the same household.

Left: 1860 census record for Frederick, Maryland. Lines 9-12 are of Peter, Hannah, Mary Margaret and Thomas. In this census the children are both teenagers. Note the difference in ages of Peter and Hannah from the 1850 census, they were both listed as forty-one years of age. Here Peter is forty-eight and Hannah fifty- three. Peter's actual age if calculated from his sale in 1826 would make him either forty-eight or forty-nine. An explanation of Hannah's two year age difference may point to her not knowing her exact age, or an error on the part of the person taking down the information.

Laid to Rest.—The funeral of Peter Frazier took place yeste-day afternoon, at 3 o'clock, from his late residence in Klinehart's alley. Services were held in Quinn s A. M. E. church, Rev. Robertson officiated, assisted by Rev. Proby, Williams and Contee. The pall-bearers were John Davis, Wm. Davis, R. E. Barnes. G B. Stanton, Richard Danher, O'Neal Gant. Interment was made at Greenmount cemetery. A. T. Rice & Sons, undertakers.

Peter Frazier's obituary. Peter died on Friday March 19, 1886. His funeral took place in his home the following Wednesday. Reprinted with the permission of the Frederick News-Post and Randall Family, LLC as published on March 26, 1886.

Maryland. Frederick County Sct.

I hereby certify that the person to whom this is given a negro man named Charles, aged about 31 years (son of Ester) five feet, seven and a half inches high, has a small scar on the left side of the forehead, is the identical negro man named Charles, manumitted by Richard Coale by deed of Manumission Recorded among the land Records of Frederick County, as appears by said Manumission & the affidavit of Col. Thos. Sappington, on file in my office. In Testimony Whereof I hereunto subscribe my name, & affix the seal of my office this first day of April 1847.

W.B. Tyler

Born Feb 17 1812 Died Feb 28 1874

Original manumission or freedom paper given to Charles Frazier in 1847. Charles would have carried this on his person at all times, without it he could have easily been jailed or sold back into slavery. That he could fall from a condition of freedom to bondage so easily surely lay on his mind daily. Though he was free, the institution of slavery continued on for countless numbers of blacks. When Charles passed on, Alice Frazier Bouldin recorded the dates of his birth and death in pencil at the bottom of the manumission.

Maryland Frederick County

I hereby certify that the person to whom this is given a negro man named Charles age about 31 years son of Ester five feet seven and a half inches high has a small scar on the left side of the forehead is the identified negro man named Charles manumitted by Richard Coale by deed of manumission recorded among the land records of Frederick County, as appears by said manumission & the affidavit of Col. Thos. Sappington, on file in my office. In testimony whereof I hereunto subscribe my name and affix the seal of my office this first day of April 1847.

WB Tyler

Charles Frazier, ca. 1860.
This tintype was perhaps Charles Frazier's only photo.

CHAPTER 3

Charles Frazier

Charles Frazier the son of Ester and brother of Peter Frazier was born in Libertytown, Maryland. Like his mother and brother he was owned by Richard Coale. Charles married Milly Butcher a slave who was also from Libertytown. During the years 1835 through 1847 six children were born to the Frazier's, George, Martha, Lizzie, Laura, Charles jr. and Lewis. Four more children were born between the years 1849-1855, bringing the Frazier's ten children in all. The first set of children, those born from 1835-1847 were born while Charles remained a slave. In 1663 The Maryland Legislature passed an act that said all children born of any negro or other slaves, shall be slaves as their fathers were for the terms of their lives. Then in 1681 an act was passed that declared that all children born of slaves would remain a slave for life, and children should follow the status of their mothers and not that of their fathers. This act ensured that each child born to the Frazier's would remain slaves in spite of Charles freedom.

Against the many cruelties and indignities of slavery Charles and Milly Frazier, living apart, answering to two separate owners, managed to stay put, and stay together.

In 1847 Charles at the age of thirty-one was free. The manumission, or freedom paper that Charles Frazier carried in his possession at all times, show that Richard Coale originated the manumission. Sometime after he was free, Charles sought employment with the man who owned his wife and children, Dr. William Tyler. In the 1850 census Charles is listed as a free inhabitant and a laborer in the Tyler household. Whose decision it was to have Charles work for William Tyler? I like to think that it was Charles and Milly, doing all that they could to keep their family together.

By 1859 the Frederick County Directory list Charles occupation as coachman. The duties of a coachman at that time would have been similar to that of a personal driver today. Doctors during this time made many home visits and Charles employed by Dr. William Tyler may have been his driver and would have traveled in and around Frederick. He would have been familiar with many of the families, both white and black, free and slave in Frederick and the surrounding areas. The stories he must have known, and witnessed would have been numerous. Charles was an extraordinary and courageous man, who instead of watching from afar became an instrument of service for his people.

Charles Frazier was a son, brother, husband, father, grandfather, provider, freemason, coachman, property owner, and one of the first black trustees of the Asbury Episcopal Methodist Church in Frederick.

There is no doubt that Charles made an impression on his family, besides his second son who was named Charles, his granddaughter Hettie named her second born son Charles, and daughter Alice named her first born son Charles. In total there have been eight males descended from Charles Frazier with the given name of Charles.

Charles Frazier died at the age of 62 on February 28, 1874, the birth date of his daughter Laura. Though no documentation of his funeral or burial were found I imagine it must have been grand, for even with the burden of slavery he was a man.

Invite to Merrill M.E. Church in 1889. It is addressed to Charles and Milly Frazier, both of whom were deceased by the time this invite was sent to them.

Photo of Old Hill Church East All Saints Street built in 1818 torn down in 1945.
The Old Hill Church was one of the churches where blacks worshipped in Frederick. The original lot was owned by William Hammond a free colored man, On January 11, 1818 it was purchased for the sum of $60 and a church was built by white people for their use, even so colored people were permitted to attend services. In 1864 Blacks purchased the church and in 1870 the church was renamed Asbury Methodist Episcopal Church. Charles Frazier was a member of this church and one of its first black trustees. The importance of the church in the lives of Blacks both free and slave cannot be ignored. Some fifty years after the free blacks in Frederick purchased the old Hill Church Charles Frazier's youngest daughter Alice Frazier Bouldin would make Asbury Church an integral part of her life in Frederick, by the time of her death in 1938 she had been a member for sixty-eight years.

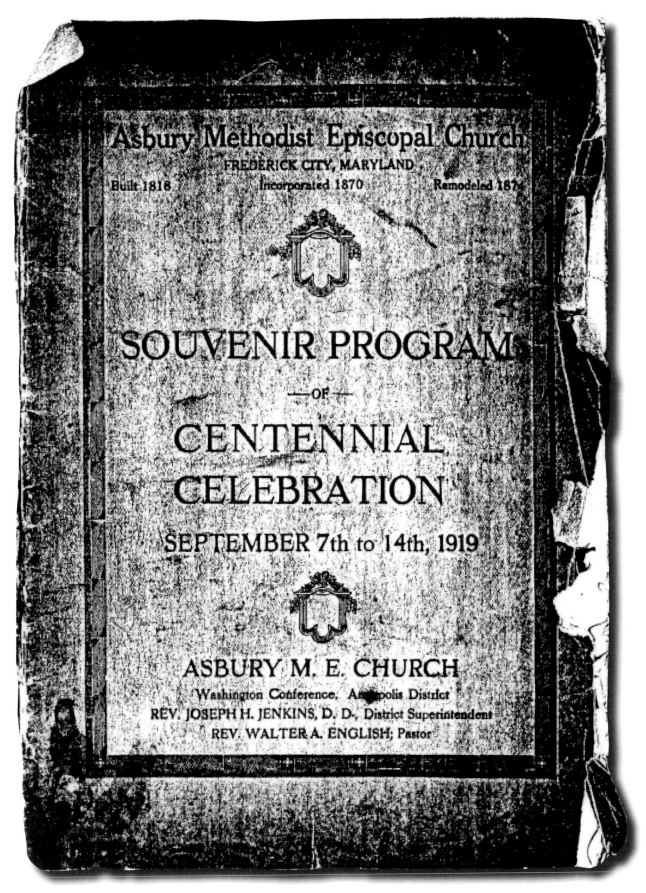

BUILT 1818   RE-BUILT 1874

Souvenir Program

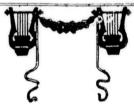

——OF THE——

Centennial Celebration

——OF——

Asbury Methodist Episcopal Church

FREDERICK CITY, MD.

REV. WALTER A. ENGLISH, Pastor

SEPTEMBER 7th to 14th, 1919

Dr. William Tyler and Mary Addison.
Photo Courtesy of Frederick Historical Society.

History of the Church

This is the oldest, and most historic Church in Frederick City. The decaying hand of time has not laid its weight so heavily upon it, that it is today a mass of ruin and desolation, but it is so well preserved that it is being used by the present generation, as a holy place in which to worship God, as did their forefathers and mothers before them.

Asbury Methodist Episcopal Church, the title by which it is now known, was built in the year of 1818. The lot was purchased for the sum of $60.00 from Mr. William Hammond a colored (free) man, Jan. 11th, 1818. The church was built by the white people for their use. Colored people were permitted to attend services. When the Church was erected, Rev. Samuel Smith was the pastor, and David Peck, James H. Harper, Nicholas Smith, Archibald Gull and Sampson Gross, were the Trustees. An addition was made to the Church in 1850. The galleries put in and the basement excavated. Was remodeled in 1874. The Church stands far back in a large yard, part of which was used for a cemetery, in which several prominent people were buried.

Among the prominent ministers who pastored here in the days of the early history of the Church is the name of Rev. Carroll. He made his home with the family of Mr. Andrew Boyd one of the First Families of Frederick, and married Mr. Boyd's daughter.

Bishop Matthew Simpson of the Methodist Episcopal Church, a staunch friend of President Abraham Lincoln preached a soul stirring sermon in this church at the death of Mr. Lincoln.

In the year of 1864, the colored people came into full possession of the Church, and Rev. Robert H. Robinson, a member of the First class of the Washington Annual Conference, was the first minister to pastor the Charge. Twenty-three pastors have served this charge since the organization of the Washington Conference in 1864, some for the second time. Out of the twenty-three ministers, only six remain, the others having died in the full triumph of faith.

The first trustees of the Church were, Francis Deacon, Charles Frazier, James Weems, Resin Contee, Alexander Robinson, Ephraim James, Solomon Snowden, Gabriel White, James Francis, John Bush, and Thomas Ramsay.

The twenty-seventh session of the Washington Conference was held at this Church March 12th, 1820. Bishop R. S. Foster, D. D., presided. This church has entertained the Conference twice.

The Church has been renovated during the pastorate of our present pastor, Rev. W. A. English. The interior beautifully frescoed, electric lights installed, the same donated by the "Boys' Club," new carpet for isles, stairway and rostrum, window shades and pulpit covered, material donated by "Girls' Club" and Ladies' Aid Society. Cement platform has taken the place of the old wooden platform at the entrance. Other improvements made by the congregation, makes the old Church look very modern in appearance. Now after a century of service we pray that the Spirit of God may hover over the place where years ago it was consecrated and made sacred unto Him.

"We love thy Church, O God.
Her walls before Thee stand,
Dear as the apple of Thine eye,
And graven on Thy hand.

"For her our tears shall fall;
For her our prayers ascend;
To her our cares and toils be given;
Till toils and cares shall end."

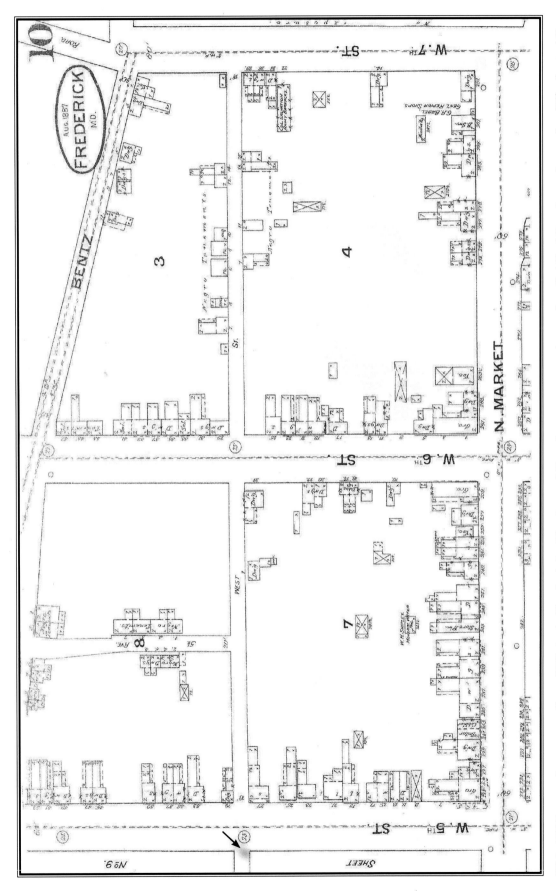

This 1887 map shows a section of Historic Frederick. Charles and Peter's property was located on Public Alley, later changed to Klineharts Alley and 5th Street. This map does not show the dwellings or tenements for that specific location. If it had it would have shown that Public Alley ran from 3rd to 5th Streets between Bentz and North Market Streets.

Frederick Herald.

SATURDAY MORNING, JANUARY 28, 1832.

entitled, be, she or they quit and finally leave this state.

Sec. 5. *And be it enacted,* That it shall not be lawful for any person or persons to give, sell or transfer, or convey, any slave or slaves to any free negro or mulatto of this state.

The bill reported by Mr. Johnson, entitled, a supplement to an act to incorporate the Fredericktown Savings Institution, passed at December session 1827, chapter 142, was taken up for consideration, read the second time, passed and sent to the senate.

The bill reported by Mr. Heard, for regulating the sales of real estate by collectors of taxes, proposes to allow the owner of any such real property, sold for taxes, to redeem the same any time within twelve months, by paying the price for which it sold, and twenty per cent. per annum interest thereon.

Congressional.

DEBATE ON THE TARIFF.

Frederick Herald, January 28, 1832, excerpt from House of Delgates Meeting in which the status of negroes, slaves, and mulattoes in the state of Maryland are discussed.

At the request of the Frederick town Savings Institution, was Recorded the following Mortgage April 27th 1853.

This Indenture, made this twenty seventh day of April in the year of our Lord one thousand eight hundred and fifty three, between Peter Frazier and Charles Frazier of Frederick County in the State of Maryland of the one part and The Frederick town Savings Institution of said County and State of the other part—Whereas the said Peter Frazier and Charles Frazier have executed their joint and serial promissory note, executed on paper duly stamped, and bearing date the 7th day of April in the year 1853, payable sixty days after date, to Lewis Ramsburg, Secretary or order for the sum of two hundred and sixty five dollars, negotiable and payable at the Frederick town Savings Institution in which said note Mountjoy B Luckett and Joseph G Miller are bound as securities, and for the purpose of fully securing the payment of said note to said Savings Institution, as also all interest which shall accrue on said note, or upon any other note or notes given in renewal of the same, they, the said Peter Frazier and Charles Frazier have agreed to execute these presents.—Now this Indenture Witnesseth, that the said Peter Frazier and Charles Frazier in consideration of the premises aforesaid, and also in consideration of the further sum of One dollar current money to them the said Peter Frazier and Charles Frazier by the said Frederick town Savings Institution in hand well and truly paid, at and before the sealing and delivery of these presents, the receipt whereof is hereby acknowledged by the said Peter Frazier and Charles Frazier, have granted, bargained and sold, released and confirmed, and by these presents do grant, bargain and sell, release and confirm unto the said Frederick town Savings Institution, All that part of a lot of ground, lying in the addition to Frederick town in the County aforesaid—Beginning for the same on the line of "Public Alley" at the west end of said lot, being the southwestern corner of the late George Kephart's lot on said Alley, and running Eastwardly 100 feet down towards Market Street, then Southwardly 39½ feet then Westwardly 100 feet to the line of "Public Alley," and then with said Alley northwardly 39½ feet

A record of the purchase of property on Public Alley in 1853. Brothers Peter and Charles Frazier obtained a mortgage for three hundred fifty-three dollars from the Fredericktown Savings Institution. Free blacks who could do so, purchased property with wages they earned and had saved for years. In rare cases free blacks were allowed to obtain bank loans or mortgages. Securing a mortgage loan during this period would have been difficult. It would have required the backing of a white citizen to help the loan go through, and to vouch for the character of the person buying the property.

At the request of Millie Frazure et al the following deed is recorded Nov 17 1876

This Deed made this 28th day of April in the Year Eighteen hundred and Seventy Four by Peter Frazure and Hannah Frazure his wife and Charles Frazure all of Frederick County Md. Witnesseth that for and in Consideration of the Natural love and affection We the the said Peter Frazure and Hannah Frazure his wife and Charles Frazure do grant unto Millie Frazure wife of Charles Frazure and Laura Frazure and Alice Frazure to hold as Joint tenants the following piece or parcel of ground Situated in Frederick City and Beginning for the same in the line of "Public Alley" at the West end of said Lot being the South western Corner of Jno Edward Gillinger's Lot on said Alley and running Eastwardly toward Market St One hundred feet then Northwardly Eighteen feet then Westwardly Seventy Six feet then Westwardly twenty four feet to the line of Public Alley then Southwardly Sixteen feet to the place of beginning It being part of the Lot or portion of ground which was Conveyed to the said Charles Frazure and Peter Frazure as tenants in common by deed from Hannah McCahan dated April 26th 1853 and recorded in Liber E. S. No 3. Folios 122 & 123 one of the Land Records of Frederick County.

Witness our hands & Seals

Test   his
C. H. Eckstein   Peter × K Frazier
Chas W. Miller   his
                           Hannah × Frazier
                                   Mark
                                        his
                           Charles × Frazier
                                   Mark

Which these Endorsed Viz:
State of Maryland Fred k. Co. Set.
I hereby Certify that on this 28th. day of April 1874 before me the Subscriber a Justice of the Peace in and for the County and State aforesaid personally appeared Peter Frazure & Hannah Frazure his wife and Charles Frazure parties to the within deed and each acknowledged the foregoing to be their act.
                           C. H. Eckstein J.P.

Public Alley property given to Milly, Laura, and Alice in 1874 as a gift. Milly who was a slave at the time of the original purchase could not legally own property.

William Downs and Laura Downs his wife do grant unto Alice Bouldin all the interest of said Laura Downs in and to all that Lot of ground situated upon "Public" or "Klinehart's" Alley in Frederick City Maryland, being the Same Lot or parcel of ground described by Metes and bounds in a deed from Peter Frazier and wife and Charles Frazier to Millie Frazier and Laura Frazier and Alice Frazier (the said Laura and Alice Frazier being now by Marriage the said Laura Downs and Alice Bouldin) bearing date the 28th day of April A.D. 1874 and duly recorded in Liber J.J. No 6 folio 316 &c One of the Land Records of Frederick County —

Witness our hands and Seals —

Test

 Jas H. Besant

    William Downs   (Seal)

    Laura her x mark Downs   (Seal)

State of Maryland Frederick County, Set:

I hereby certify that on this 15th day of October in the year Eighteen hundred and Eighty four before me a Justice of the Peace in and for the County and State aforesaid personally appeared William Downs and Laura Downs his wife, and each acknowledged the foregoing deed to be their respective act.

      James H. Besant J.P.

In 1884 Alice Frazier Bouldin bought Laura's share of the Public Alley property for $125.

Headstone of Charles Frazier, Fairview Cemetery, Frederick, Maryland. Still visible, though barely are the masonic square and compass at the top of the stone, Charles Frazier's name in the middle and at the bottom the word "Born. Fortunately the Frazier's left behind several documents which show the date of birth and death of Charles Frazier.

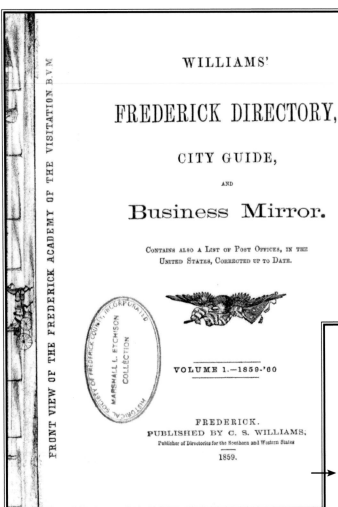

Copy of Frederick Directory for years 1859-1860. Frederick Historical Society.

Line 8: Charles Frazier. Line15: Peter Frazier. The asterisk in front of the name identifies the person as colored. Though Peter did not have his occupation listed next to his name, only those individuals who were free and employed had their names included in this directory.

Milly's Symphony

I PLANT YOU.
I SING YOU ALL AROUND.
IN MY BELLY
A SONG OF LIFE AND LOVE.

I RECORD YOU, EVEN THOUGH THEY SAY NO.
SO THAT YOU WILL BE REMEMBERED AS MINE.

YOUR NAMES REPEATED IN TIME
A LINE DEFINED AS
FAMILY.

Patricia Washington

CHAPTER 4

Milly Butcher Frazier

According to documents left by Alice Frazier Bouldin, her mother Milly Butcher was born in Libertytown, Maryland, and before being owned by William Tyler she belonged to a Mrs. Rice of Libertytown. Census records state that Milly and both of her parents were all born in the state of Maryland. Though there has been no identification of either parent or sibling existing in Milly's life, several photographs of at least three Butcher tombstones were found in the William O. Lee Jr. collection at the Frederick Historical Society, and there was a Mary V. Butcher who witnessed Alice Frazier Bouldin's will in 1934. How Milly Butcher was related to the people whose tombstones appear in the pictures or Mary V. Butcher is not known. The tombstones have been quite difficult to follow, and Mary V. Butcher may have been a niece or grand niece of Milly's.

THE BABIES

Charles and Milly had seven daughters and none were named after Milly. *"The absence of infant girls named for their mothers appears to have been a distinctive slave practice."* Herbert G. Guttman, 1977. This practice was in contrast to that of their owners, who during that same time period often named daughters for their mothers. Instead Milly named two daughters for a dead sibling, this is called necronymic naming, where a child is named for a dead relative. Milly did this twice, in 1851 she named a daughter Laura after a Laura who had been born in 1843 and died in 1845. Then in 1853 she named a daughter Elizabeth for another daughter who had been born in 1840 and died in 1852. The origins of necronymic naming within the Frazier family is not known. It could have simply been Milly's way of remembering her deceased children. It may also have been a practice that was developed within the larger slave community she was a part of.

Both baby Laura who died at the age of two years and baby Rachel who died at the age of six months had their births and deaths recorded by Milly in her small book. A cause of death or burial place was not included in these records. If Milly noted the burial places of her children that information no longer exists and was not found in the family papers.

In later years Milly extended her role as mother to include the daughter of Martha who would have been little more than a year old when Martha passed away. In 1870 Hettie born in 1861 was in the household of her grandparents and remained with her grandmother until Milly's death in 1880. Milly's refusal to lose any of her children through slavery or death is a testimony of her role as mother, protector, and nurturer, regardless of the circumstances she was forced to live by.

Tintype of Milly Butcher Frazier.

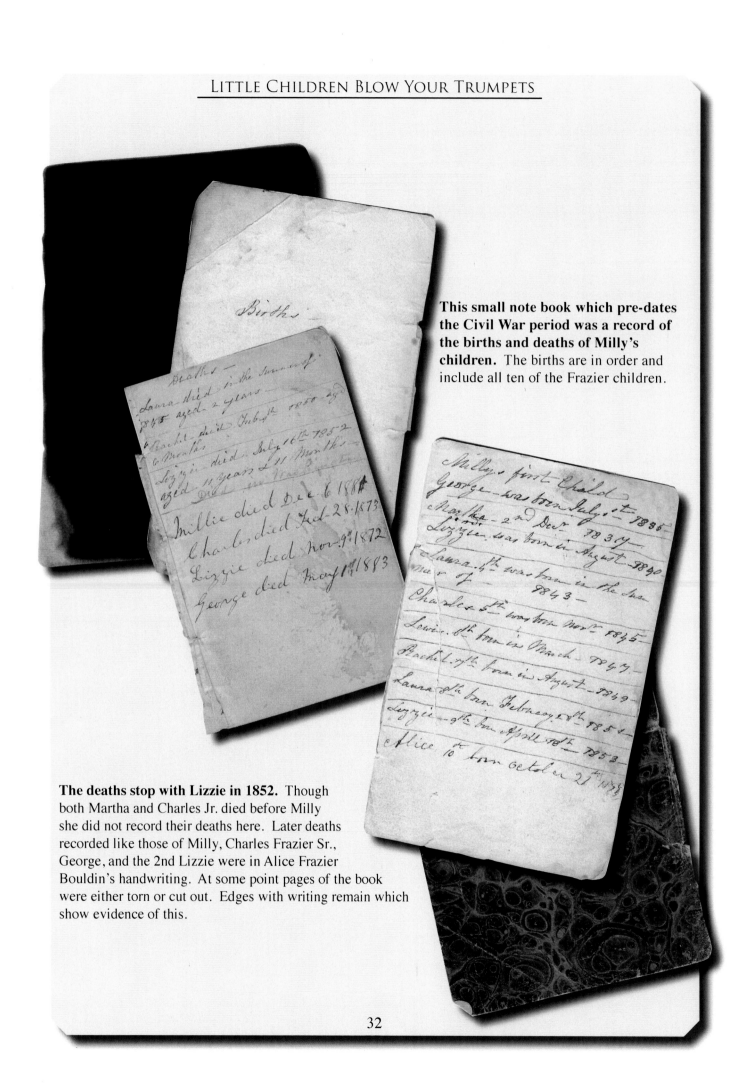

This small note book which pre-dates the Civil War period was a record of the births and deaths of Milly's children. The births are in order and include all ten of the Frazier children.

The deaths stop with Lizzie in 1852. Though both Martha and Charles Jr. died before Milly she did not record their deaths here. Later deaths recorded like those of Milly, Charles Frazier Sr., George, and the 2nd Lizzie were in Alice Frazier Bouldin's handwriting. At some point pages of the book were either torn or cut out. Edges with writing remain which show evidence of this.

Slave mothers upon learning of the approaching sale of their children would take a piece of hair, or clothing that belonged to that child. Children sold away were often never seen again, and this physical memory would be all that they would ever have of that child.

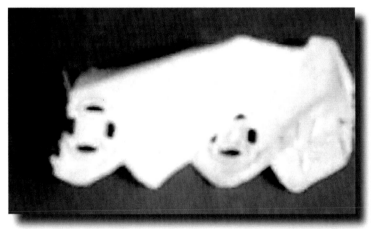

Found between separate pages of the family Bible were two small pieces of cloth. One is a blue and white gingham, the other is a white lace. The size, type, and estimated age of each fabric point to one of the Frazier girls. My guess is they were pieces of dresses worn by Martha who was sold before age fifteen, and the 1st Lizzie who was sold away before age eleven.

White fabric possibly taken from a dress, now yellow in color was found in the family bible.

A piece of blue and white gingham fabric also found between pages of the family Bible. Gingham was often used to make clothing for the slaves.

Milly Butcher Frazier.
This type of photo pin became popular in the mid 1870's.

Milly Frazier wife of Charles Frazier died Dec. 6, 1880, 62 years.

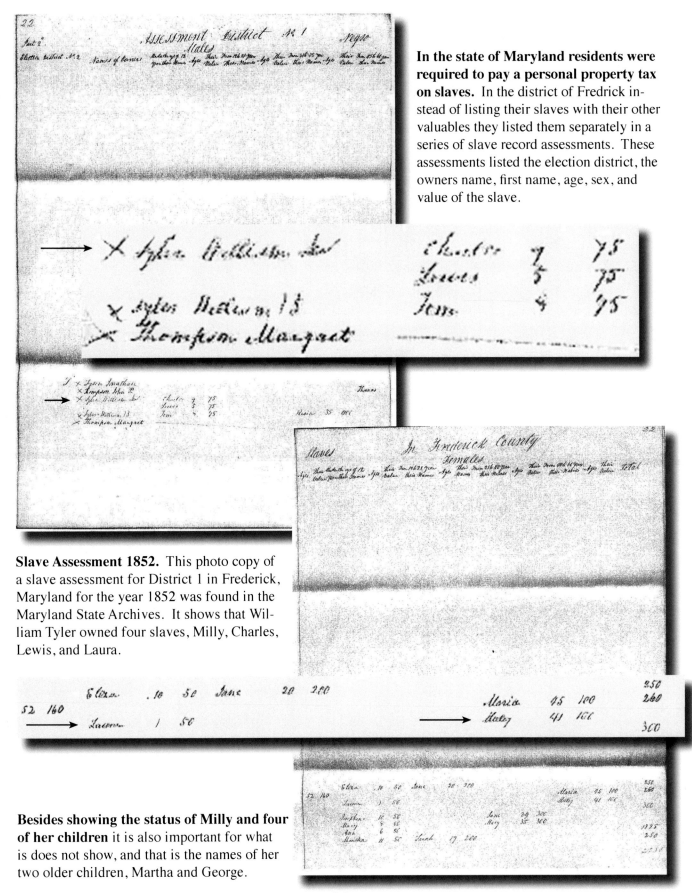

In the state of Maryland residents were required to pay a personal property tax on slaves. In the district of Fredrick instead of listing their slaves with their other valuables they listed them separately in a series of slave record assessments. These assessments listed the election district, the owners name, first name, age, sex, and value of the slave.

Slave Assessment 1852. This photo copy of a slave assessment for District 1 in Frederick, Maryland for the year 1852 was found in the Maryland State Archives. It shows that William Tyler owned four slaves, Milly, Charles, Lewis, and Laura.

Besides showing the status of Milly and four of her children it is also important for what is does not show, and that is the names of her two older children, Martha and George.

This record of sale was found in the Land Records for Frederick, Maryland. It states that a man named William Perry who is in debt to a man called Alfred Trail has sold off whatever he had in value in order to make payment on the debt. In this sale he has decided to sell off his seventeen year old female slave named Milly, who Dr. William Tyler and Gideon Bantz purchase.

Sale of Milly to Gideon Bantz and Dr. William Tyler, 1823. Though this sale is of a Milly in the year 1823, it may not be Milly Butcher Frazier. First, the person who originated the sale was named William Perry, the name Rice does not appear in this document at all. However, this may be a result of a sale made from Mrs. Rice to William Perry. Next is the age of Milly as it appeared in the sale, seventeen. This age would make her birth year 1806, contradicting the age found on her tombstone which is sixty-two.

456

consideration of one Dollar current money to me in hand paid I have granted, bargained and sold and by these presents do grant bargain and sell unto the said Doctor William Tyler and Gideon Bantz their Executors administrators and assigns, one negro Girl named Milly now about Seventeen years of age and now in my possession To Have and to hold the said negro Girl Milly to the said Doctor William Tyler and Gideon Bantz their Executors administrators & assigns forever and I the said William Perry for myself my heirs Executors and administrators the aforesaid negro Girl Milly to the said Doctor William Tyler and Gideon Bantz their Executors administrators and assigns against me the said William Perry my Executors and administrators and against all and every person and persons whomsoever shall and will warrant and forever defend by these presents provided nevertheless that in Case I the said William Perry shall pay and satisfy unto the said Alfred Trail or to his Executors administrators or assigns the said sum of two hundred Dollars current money with interest for the same on or before the Eighteenth day of March in the year Eighteen hundred and Twenty four & indemnify and Save harmless the said Doctor William Tyler & Gideon Bantz as my securities in said note then this bill of Sale and every matter and thing therein expressed shall be void and of none effect and the said Doctor William Tyler and Gideon Bantz by a good and sufficient release of Sale duly executed and acknowledged according to law shall release & reconvey to me the said William Perry the said negro Girl Milly it being the true intent and meaning thereof that the said negro Girl Milly is mortgaged by me the said William Perry to secure & indemnify the said Doctor William Tyler and Gideon Bantz as my securities in the note aforesaid In Witness whereof I the said William Perry have hereunto Set my hand and affixed my Seal this Twenty first day of March in the year one thousand eight hundred and twenty three. Signed Sealed & Delivered in presence of

John I McCulley

Wm Perry — [seal]

Which is thus endorsed vizt Maryland Frederick County Set on this 21st day of March 1823 Before me one of the Justices of the peace in and for said County appears William Perry and acknowledges the foregoing

If she was sixty-two in 1880 she would have been born in the year 1818, not 1806. Alone these two dates may lead one to think that the Milly in the sale was not Milly Butcher Frazier. But the 1852 slave assessment record listed her age as forty-one, giving her a birth year of 1811, falling between the dates of 1806 and 1818. Years later, an 1870 census recorded her age as fifty-four, which would make her birth year 1816. Finally, this was a time when black people had little or no say about what information was documented on their behalf, and her owner may have guessed her age. This I am quite sure occurred more often than not and could be the reason for the discrepancies in age for Milly Butcher Frazier. Also there is a chance she like many slaves did not know her day or year of birth. This effect of slavery must have remained with Milly throughout her life, and may have been the motivation for her documentation of her own children's births and deaths.

Family Bible. This large Bible was the property of Charles and Milly Frazier. It was likely to have been purchased or given to the Frazier's shortly after its printing, as this edition was published in 1861.

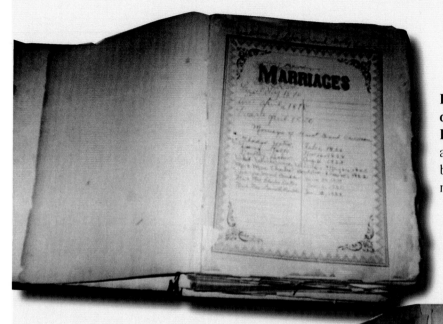

In addition to noting the births, deaths, and marriages of the Frazier's it also contains the births and marriages of the Bouldin's beginning with Charles Bouldin's marriage to Sara Frances in 1903.

Several of the cartes de visite photos that appear in this book were found in the family and marriage section at the back of the Bible.

The death of Sara Frances Bouldin, in 1933 was also documented in the Bible.

Forget not, O my brothers,
how we fought
In No Man's Land that peace might come again!

Forget not, O my brothers,
how we gave
Red blood to save the freedom of the world!

Fenton Johnson
1888-1958

CHAPTER 5

The Frazier Brothers

GEORGE FRAZIER JULY 1, 1835- MAY 1, 1883

CHARLES FRAZIER NOVEMBER 2, 1845- 1866

LEWIS FRAZIER MARCH 1847- 1875

George Frazier was the first born child of Milly and Charles, he was not named after his father, but may have been named for a close relative. By 1852 he was no longer with his mother, and following the buying and selling practices of slave owners he may have been sold off before the age of sixteen. He did not have any children and no record of marriage was found. The family must have known where George was as they did record his date of his death. By 1883 both parents were deceased and buried in Greenmount Cemetery, George may have also been buried there.

Charles Frazier was the second son, and fifth child. Shortly after his birth he was baptized at All Saints Church in Frederick. At the time of his death Charles was nineteen years of age. There were no records of marriage, or children for Charles. I thought at first that he might have gone to fight in the Civil War, but a search of war records came up empty. The last living record of Charles was documented in 1852 when he appeared in the slave assessment record with his mother and several siblings. Lewis Frazier the third son and sixth child like his two older brothers did not marry or have children.

What happened to the Frazier brothers? Why didn't any of them have children, or get married? I cannot imagine that they did either, as all marriages and grandchildren were written down in the family bible, and the Frazier brothers would have been no exception. I have spent hours imagining numerous scenarios that could have befallen them but have found no proof to substantiate that any of them ever happened. I imagine that one or the other could have run away and this would be one reason why no records, census or other were found. As I searched Civil War records, including receiving the packet of one Lewis Frazier whom I believed was my Lewis, I found that many colored soldiers enlisted from places other than their home towns. Some used aliases instead of their own given names, as they could have been run-aways, and needed to be wary of owners and bounty hunters who were trying to capture and return them to slavery. Still others changed their ages in order to either become younger or older on paper. A young male slave who was healthy and had a skill was a valuable slave and could bring both the seller and buyer a large sum of money. For this reason I cannot dismiss that either of the brothers were sold out of state but somehow were able to keep in touch. What occurred in the lives of these three Frazier men, that two of them lived some years after the end of slavery but left no record of their existence I often ponder.

Black families free and slave were sometimes allowed to attend church. This record shows that the Frazier's baptized their children as early as 1843.

14   *Western Maryland Genealogy*

Fitzhugh, Isabella Hudson, dau. of Peregrine & Marg., b. 15 Jan. 1843; bp. 14
    July 1845

Fitzhugh, Sarah Margaretta, dau. of Peregrine & Margaret, b. 16 May 1846;
    bp. 15 Feb. 1847 at Catoctin Furnace

Fout, Mary Ann, dau. Otho & Catherine, b. 31 Oct. 1831; bp. 26 Feb. 1832

Fowler, Charles Cornelius, son Bartholomew Thomas & Precilla Ann, b. 18
    Oct. 1826; bp. 6 May 1827 [two entries]

Fowler, Mariann, dau. Thomas & Priscilla, b. 25 Sept.; bp. 26 Dec. 1824

Fowler, Samuel Albert, son Bartholomew & Priscilla Ann, b. 21 Feb.; bp. 22
    March (3 Oct.?) 1830

Frazier, Catherine Eliza, dau. Henry & Elizabeth, b. 8 Oct. 1826

Frazier, Charles, col., son of Charles & Milly, b. 3 Dec. 1844; bp. 27 Jan. 1846

Frazier, Mary Margaret, dau. of Peter & Anna, col., ill, b. 28 Aug.; bp. 21
    Dec. 1843

French, Ford J., adult, 20 June 1855

Funk, Sarah Jane, age 8m 3d, dau. of Henry & Nancy, bp. 25 Dec. 1846 at
    Catoctin Furnace

Gaither, Anna Elizabeth, dau. Stuart & Margaret, b. 24 June 1828; bp. 14
    June 1829

Gaither, Caroline Augusta, dau. Stuart & Margaret, bp. 25 June 1826

Gaither, Juliana, dau. Stuart & Margaret, b. 21 May; bp. 17 Oct. 1824

Gaither, Sarah Jane, dau. same, b. 23 May; bp. 3 Oct. 1830

Gaither, Stuart, son Henry & Elizth, b. 14 Aug. 1785; bp. 1817

Gaither, Stuart, son of Stuart & Margt., 8 July 1832

Gales, William Henry, col. son of William & Ann, b. 6 July 1833

Gauronski, Leon William Dudley, age 9m, at Rice's Hotel, parents about to
    go from Frederick, 30 Sept. 1851

Gibson, Fanny Hite, age 2½y, and William Waters, age 3m, 8 Dec. 1850

Gibson, James, son of Dr. & [blank], 27 April 1856

Goldsborough, Bridget Poe, ill, dau. of Dr. Charles & Amelia, b. 3 April; bp.
    2 July 1845

Goldsborough, Charles Worthington, son of Dr. Charles & Amelia, b. 29
    Nov. 1841, bp. 30 June 1843

Goldsborough, Edward, son of Ed. & Mary, b. 28 Feb.; bp. 11 Aug. 1838

Goldsborough, Edwd. Y., son of Ed. & Mary, b. Dec. 1839; bp. 3 March 1841

Goldsborough, Eliza Margaret, dau. of Dr. Edw. & Margt., b. 10 April; bp.
    21 June 1845

Goldsborough, Margaret Eliza, infant dau. of Dr. Edward & Margaret, bp.
    21 Aug. 1833

Goldsborough, Mary Catherine, dau. Edward Y. & Margaret, b. 7 Oct. 1827;
    bp. 22 Oct. 1828

Charles Frazier and cousin Mary Margaret Frazier baptismal from published
compilation of All Saints Church records.

This photo was taken by Josiah Marken a Frederick photographer in the middle 1860's. While no definitive identification of the young man in this photo has been made, the approximate date of the picture point to either George or Lewis Frazier. He appears older than Charles Frazier jr.'s nineteen years.

We were not free,
our tawny hands were tied;

But Belgium's plight
and Serbia's woes

We shared

Fenton Johnson
1888-1958

CHAPTER 6

Martha Frazier & Hettie Frazier

*M*artha Frazier was born December 2, 1837, in either Libertytown or Frederick, Maryland. She was the second child born to Charles and Milly. From her birth in 1837 to her death in 1862 her whereabouts are unknown. Like her older brother George she was sold away by the time the 1852 slave assessment was taken. Martha does not appear in any records I was able to locate. A search of slave assessments for all districts in Frederick and surrounding areas failed to produce either Martha or her brother George who would have been 15 and 17 in 1852. Judging from Charles Frazier's life after freedom, and Milly's documentation of her children's birth and death, Martha was not too far away from her parents. Martha would have been the first daughter to be sold away, and may have been taken to the same place as her brother George. At one point Charles Frazier's occupation as a coachman, and the fact that he was a free man would have given him the opportunity to either see, or visit Martha and relay messages back and forth between mother and daughter. Charles and Milly had three grandchildren, the first being, Henrietta or Hettie. Martha gave birth to Hettie on July 21, 1861, she did not marry and Hettie's father is unknown. Martha died in 1862 leaving behind an infant Hettie, who sometime during slavery or right after was in the care of her grandparents, and not sold away. In the early 1890's she married Henry Williams, and they had seven children, Lewis and Charles who both died as infants, Arie their only daughter, John, Thomas, Franklin and Marshall. By 1910 Hettie was a widow, and in later years she remarried to a man named George West.

Hettie was an important part of the Frazier family, in several letters between Alice Frazier Bouldin and her granddaughter Alice Bouldin, either Hettie, or several of her children are mentioned. For most of her young years she lived and worked in Frederick. In a 1919 Asbury Church Bulletin she is listed as one of its members. In 1910 she appears in a Frederick News article as a victim of a fire. She was living on Ice Street when the property caught fire, causing her to lose her place of residence and all of her personal property.

Hettie Frazier Circa. 1880

J. DAVIS BYERLY,

SUCCESSOR TO

JACOB BYERLY,

Photographer,

29 N. MARKET ST.

FREDERICK, MD.

☞ All styles of Frames always on hand

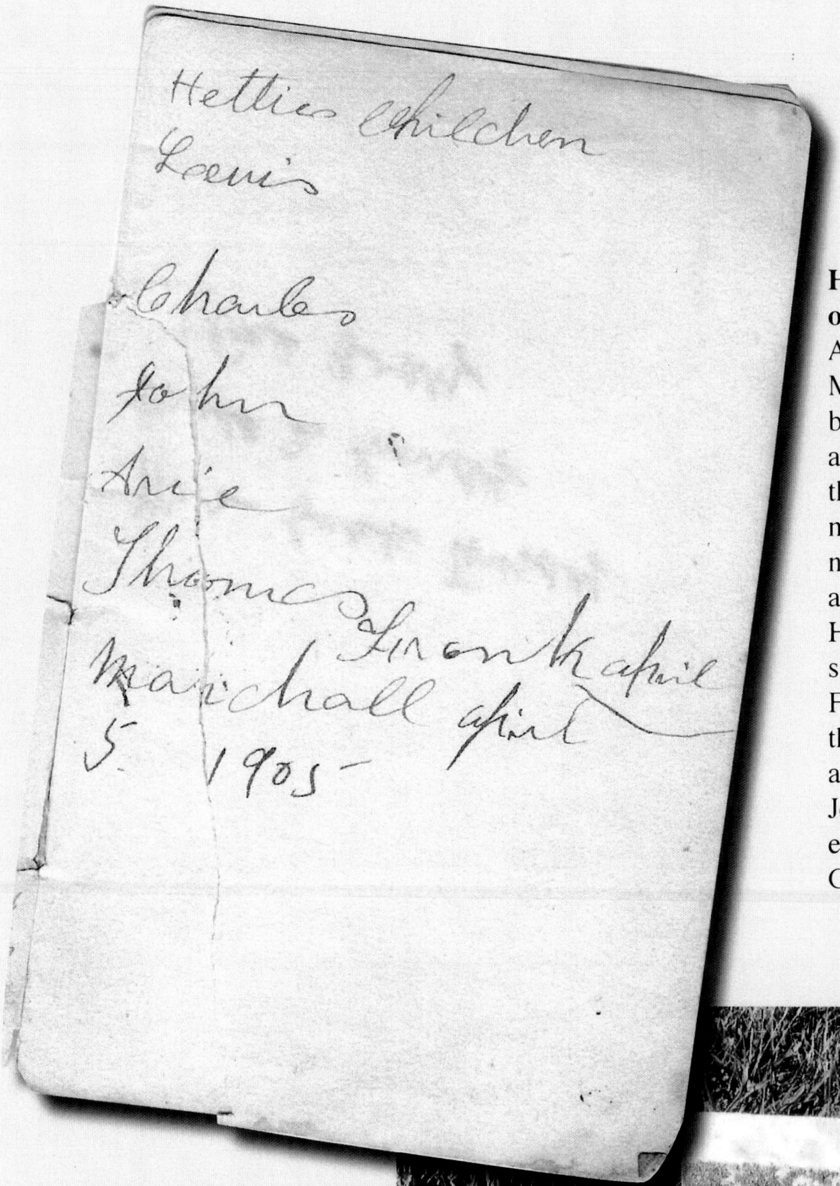

Hettie's children
Lewis

Charles

John

Arie

Thomas Frank April

Marshall April
5 1905-

Hettie's children, listed in order of birth: Lewis, Charles, John, Arie, Thomas, Franklin, and Marshall, who Alice noted was born April 5, 1905. Both Lewis and Charles died as infants. Arie the only girl left Frederick and moved to Reading, Pennsylvania. Hettie passed away in 1935 at the home of her daughter Arie. Hettie's remaining five children survived her. Hettie is buried in Fairview Cemetery in Frederick, three of her children, Arie, Thomas and Marshall are also buried there. John is buried in St. John's Cemetery and Franklin in Mt. Olivet Cemetery in Frederick.

HATTIE WEST
1861 - 1935

Illustration depicts grieving parents whose child has been sold away from them. Little girl mourns for those she may never see again. Danielle West 2009.

CHAPTER 7
Elizabeth "First Lizzie" Frazier

Born in 1840 Lizzie was the third child of Charles and Milly.

When she was around eight years of age she was sent to live with Dr. William Tyler's newly married daughter Susan. Susan Tyler married Orlando Peck on April 3, 1849. Slave trading tore apart families in a way that folks today would never truly understand.

Jennifer Hill a former slave gave this description: "Some people think that slaves had no feeling that they bore their children as animals bear their young and that there was no heart-break when the children were torn from their parents or the mother taken from her brood to toil for a master in another state. But that isn't so. The slaves loved their families even as the Negroes love their own today and the happiest time of their lives was when they could sit at their cabin doors when the day's work was done and sang the old slave songs, "Swing Low Sweet Chariot," "Massa's in the Cold, Cold Ground, " and "Nobody Know What Trouble I've Seen."

Children learned these songs and sang them only as a Negro child could. That was the slave's only happiness, a happiness that for many of them did not last."

For Lizzie and her family indeed it did not last.

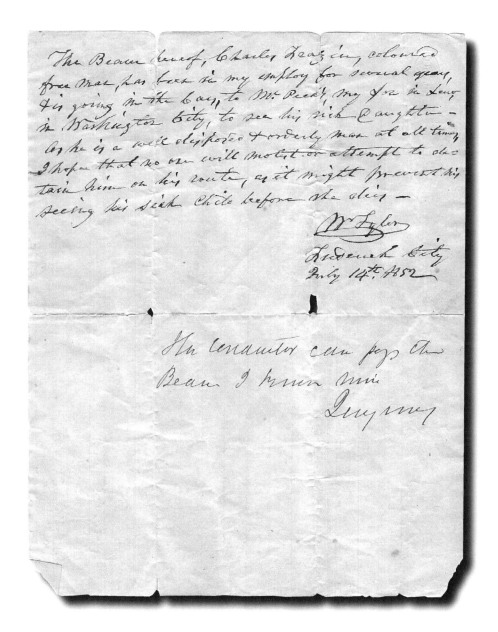

This original letter, over one hundred and fifty years old was written for the purpose of securing Charles Frazier's safety as he travelled to Washington to see his sick daughter Lizzie. Without this letter travelling outside of Frederick City could have resulted in some type of injury coming to Charles. Besides the piece of fabric found in the Bible this letter was all that the Frazier's had left of their Lizzie. I often wonder if Charles made it there on time to see her, and what his emotions were on what must have felt like a very long journey to Washington. Lizzie died July 16, 1852.

The bearer hereof, Charles Frazier is colored freeman, has been in my employ for several years, and is going in the day to Mr. Peck my son-law in Washington City to see his sick daughter as he is a well disciplined and orderly man at all times I hope that no one will molest or attempt to detain him on his route as it might prevent him from seeing his sick daughter before she dies.

Wm Tyler, Frederick City
July 14th, 1852

Deaths

DIED.—In this city on the 4th inst., at the residence of her father, Dr. William Tyler, Mrs. *Susan E. Peck*, wife of O. S. X Peck, Esq, of Washington city, in the 28th year of her age.

Attractive in her person, winning in her manners and singularly amiable in her disposition, the life of this lady was a continual pleasure to her friends. But when disease bound her to the bed of sickness, then it was, that the loveliness of her character appeared in its serenest beauty. During month after month of the greatest suffering, her meek spirit uttered not a murmur, but submissive to the will of God, she cheered by her words of friendship those whose friendly office it was to comfort her. And at the last sad scene, when friends had gathered around in one throng of weeping affection, her mild spirit tranquil in its religious hopes, bid farewell to those she loved best with a smile that lingered and faded in the shades of death. The flower has fallen, and the grace of its earthly fashion has perished, but it blooms anew, in a land where it is wooed by zephyrs of love.

Obituary found in the Frederick Examiner 1853, confirm that William Tyler's daughter married an Orlando Peck. The letter written by Dr. Tyler in 1852 said that Charles Frazier was en-route to the Peck home in Washington. The couple married in 1849, Lizzie might have been a wedding present. Susan Peck's death of disease shortly after that of Lizzie make it feasible that young Lizzie may have succumbed to the same illness.

Report of Deaths in Frederick city, for July, 1852.

Convulsions 3; Consumption 1; Abdominal Abscess 1; Cholera Infantum 7; Dysentery 3; Tonsillitis 1; Fracture of Cranium 1; Rheumatic Carditis 1.

62 years 1; 26 years 3; 20 years 1; 4 years 1; 3 years 1; 2 years 1; 19 months 1; 18 months 2; 12 months 1; 8 months 1; 6 months 2; 5 months 1; 11 days 1; 14 days 1.

Males 14; Females 4—Whites 17; Colored 1; Slaves 1—Total 18. By order of the Board,
SAMUEL TYLER, M. D., Sec'y.
aug. 11   JAMES BARTGIS, Mayor.

I. O. of O. F.

THE members of Mount Olive Encampment notified to attend their regular meet...

Frederick Academy.

THE patrons of this Institution, are respectfully informed that the duties will be resumed, on MONDAY, August 30th, 1852.
aug. 11—2t.

SELECT HIGH SCHOOL,

S. E. corner of Market & Patrick Sts.

HAVING retired from Public School, No. 71, of Frederick City, of which the undersigned was principal for the last 6 years, he takes great pleasure in returning his grateful acknowledgments to his former patrons and

Each rise of sun
or setting of the moon.

So when the bugle blast
had called us forth

We went not like the surly brute of yore
But, as the Spartan,
proud to give the world

The freedom
that we never knew nor shared.

Fenton Johnson
1888-1958

CHAPTER 8
Frazier Family Photos

Mary Addison Page, 4 years old daughter of Nannie Tyler Page and Walker Page. Circa 1864. This photo was found in the Frazier family album, an identical photo can also be found in the Frederick historical Library as part of the Tyler Page Collection.

Nancy (Nannie) Tyler Page, Laura Frazier and Mary Addison Page. Nannie was the daughter of Dr. William Tyler and Mary Addison Tyler. Born in 1851 Laura Frazier was the eighth child born to Charles and Milly Frazier. Photo Courtesy of Frederick Historical Society.

Picture postcard of young man all dressed up, wearing his bowler hat tilted slightly to the left, ca. 1910, Frederick, Maryland. This photo was found among Alice Frazier Bouldin's documents.

Unidentified young man,
photographer unknown, ca 1890.

Tintype of man believed to George Bouldin, husband of Alice Frazier.
He is wearing the uniform of a fraternal organization called the Odd fellows.

African American men joined Odd Fellow lodges that were chartered by The Grand United Order of Odd Fellows, founded in 1843. The original charter had to come from the Grand Lodge in Manchester, England because the white odd fellows would not support black chapters. Black Fraternal orders like the Odd Fellows were popular long before the Civil War as places where blacks could perfect their business and economic skills as well as socialize.

Tintype of unidentified woman,
photographer unknown, ca. 1895.

Large Charcoal Portrait of woman,
ca. 1890

Unidentified toddler sitting on chair with hands folded. This tintype was found in the small family album along with Charles and Milly's photos. It could be any one of the Frazier children or grand-children. Once Tintypes were developed in the mid 1850's they continued to be popular through the twentieth century, and was the photo of choice for many blacks because they were inexpensive to purchase.

This unidentified young girl was possibly a daughter of one of Alice Frazier Bouldin's acquaintances. Maybe not family, but important enough for her photograph to be placed in the family Bible alongside those of the Frazier women. The back of the photograph states that it was taken by PErly Photographic Studio, 15 Hill Street, Newry, next to the R.C. Cathedral. Newry is the fourth largest city in Northern Ireland, and the Roman Catholic Cathedral mentioned was built in 1829. This photo appears to have been taken sometime in the early twentieth century.

Tintype photo of Laura Frazier Downs circa 1870 **Tintype photo of a young William Downs** circa 1870.

These are the earliest photos found of both William and Laura. The nesting table which appears in both photos seem to be identical telling us that the photos were likely to have been taken by the same photographer on the same day. In William's picture the photographer must have prompted him to lie open the book to give one the impression that he had received an education. I don't think William Downs needed this touch at all. His posture, expression, and dress all suggest a very dignified and educated man all by themselves. The fact that the book's in Laura's photograph remained closed speak to a time when women were not expected to have an education at least not one that would lead to positions of leadership or power.

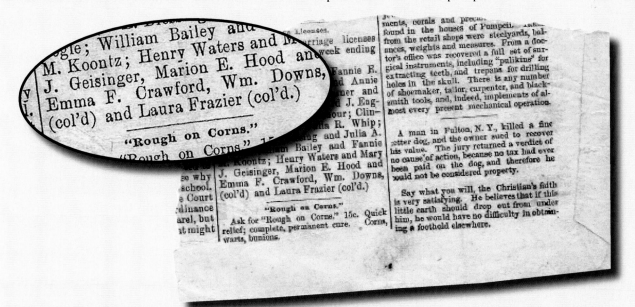

Original news clipping taken from the pages of the Frederick News Post, and found between the pages of the family Bible. It announces that William Downs, (col'd) and Laura Frazier (col'd) applied for a marriage license the week ending March 29th. Laura the eldest of the three surviving Frazier daughters married at the age of thirty to Williams Downs who was thirty-two years old. Laura and William married on April 11, 1883.

CHAPTER 9

Laura Frazier & William Downs

Laura Frazier was the fifth daughter. She was named for an older sister who died years earlier. Laura's birth begins the second chapter of the Frazier family. By the time she arrived in February 1851 her mother had been in bondage for more than forty years. No record of sale was found for Laura. She may have lived with her mother and two younger siblings until the slaves were freed, at which time she would have been fourteen years of age. However, this idealistic conclusion of what may have occurred to Laura prior to emancipation conflicts with William Tyler's past generosity toward the Frazier children. At least three of the children were sold off or given away to family members, and though no proof has been found to show that Laura shared this fate, the likelihood of it happening is more for than against. Laura did not appear in the census records taken right after slavery, her whereabouts during this year, 1870 are unknown. According to an 1880 record Laura age twenty-eight was living in the home of her mother Milly along with her two nieces Hettie and Mary. Whatever her circumstances might have been from birth through the end of slavery she maintained close ties to her family, community, and church. This same 1880 census provides the only documented record of employment for Laura, it states that she was a domestic, however she did not live in the home of her employers.

The first record of William Downs was found in the land records for Frederick, Maryland. In 1880 William Downs purchased the western half of a lot of ground which was situated on the southern side of West All Saints Street for the sum of seven hundred fifty dollars. This property known as 168 West All Saints Street, remained in the family until 1938 the year Alice Frazier Bouldin passed away. Whether William Downs was originally from Frederick, or came to reside there after slavery's end is unknown. No family or other relatives have been traced. A look through civil war enlistment records for Maryland list two men with the last name of Downs. The first, Isaac Downs enlisted into the 30th USCI from Frederick, the second Charles Downs enlisted in the 4th USCI from the Middletown area. Other than the three, no record of any other persons with the surname Downs in Frederick or its surrounding areas have been found.

In April 1883 Laura Frazier married William Downs. It appears that Laura married a man who was very much like her own father Charles Frazier. Both William Downs and Laura were very connected to their community, as well as being lifelong members of Asbury Methodist Episcopal Church on West All Saints, Laura was an Eastern Star, and William a member of various organizations, including the Fredericktonian

Lodge #12, F.A.M. Select Chapter No. 8, and the Order of Nazarites to name a few. They did not have any children of their own, but their love of Alice and nephew Charles was evident through the many photos and letters they left behind. While William Downs was employed at the Maryland School for The Deaf for many years, there was no record of Laura working outside of the house other than the domestic work she had done as a teenager shortly after emancipation, as a matter of fact in census records she appeared in after 1900 her occupation is listed as that of a housewife. In July 1914 Laura died, she was sixty-three.

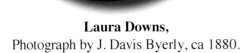

A daily log kept by the Maryland School For The Deaf documented William Downs illness and subsequent death: William suffered a heart attack on the morning of June 18, 1929 in the school's wood room. He was given first aid and escorted home by two other employees. On June 28th an employee visited the home and found that William was gravely ill, and noted that she did not think he would recover. On June 30th at 8:45 in the morning William passed away at his home. Several employees from the school visited the home but remarked that, "there seemed nothing that they could do for them save send some flowers." On July 2nd William Downs was laid to rest after an elaborate service at the church which lasted from 2:30-4:30. Employees from the school attended the funeral.

Laura Downs,
Photograph by J. Davis Byerly, ca 1880.

Laura Downs,
Photographer W.C. Bell, ca 1900.

Laura Downs, photograph by J. Davis Byerly, ca. 1885. Laura Downs was a member of the Queen Ester No. 2 Chapter of Eastern Star. Though the medallion she is wearing is unrecognizable it is likely related to her membership in the organization.

The post card is addressed to Laura Downs.
The handwriting is that of Alice Frazier Bouldin who was residing in New York City at the time, she sent this photo postcard of her three grandchildren to her sister Laura in Frederick, Maryland.

Picture Postcard sent to Laura Downs, from left to right: Alice Bouldin, Laura Bouldin, and Gladys Bouldin. Laura Bouldin, the third and last Laura, great granddaughter of Charles and Milly Frazier died at the age of two years. Circa 1907.

Portrait of sisters Laura and Alice,
Photographer unknown, ca 1870.

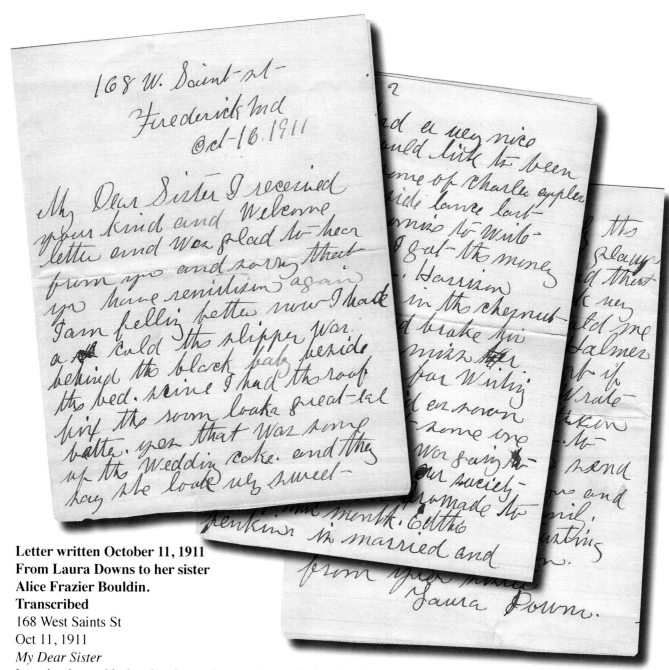

**Letter written October 11, 1911
From Laura Downs to her sister
Alice Frazier Bouldin.
Transcribed**

168 West Saints St
Oct 11, 1911

My Dear Sister

I received your kind and welcome letter and was glad to hear from you and sorry that you have reniltism (?) again. I am feeling better now I have a cold the dipper was behind the black baby beside the bed. Since I had the roof fixed the room looks a great deal better. Yes that was some of the wedding cake and they say she look very sweet and she had a very nice wedding I would like to been there to eat some of Charles apples.

Hettie had her side lance last week. Arie promises to write, but first yes I got the money for the society- Harrison Frazier was up in the chestnut tree and fell and broke his leg. Mrs. Bailey miss you very much for writing for her. She said as soon as she gets someone to writ for her she was going to answer your letter. Our society wanted to have a apron made the 26th of this month. Edthie Jenkins is married and is getting along very nicely. Mrs. Friends miss you and Gladys very much and very glad you do not have to work very hard. Mrs. Burgess told me last month that Mr. Halmer was dead and I thought if it was so you would wrote and told me. Ma-Elkin will have to-morrow to spend a week. William send his best- regard to you and Gladys and all the family. Excuse long delay trusting to hear from you soon.

From your sister Laura Downs

William Downs and Alice Frazier Bouldin, ca. 1929. This photo was taken on the grounds of the Maryland School For The Deaf. Both William and Alice were in the employ of the school for many years. Standing behind them are the schools superintendant, Ignatius Bjorlee and his wife Cornelia Bjorlee.

Obituary for Laura Downs Reprinted with the permission of the Frederick News-Post and Randall Family, LLC as published in June 1915.

THE WORK OF DEATH

MRS. WILLIAM H. DOWNS.

Mrs. Laura Downs, wife of William H. Downs colored, died last evening at her home on West All Saints' street, of general debility, aged 63 years. She was a member of Asbury M. E. Church and the Order of the Eastern Star. She is survived by her husband and one sister, Mrs. Alice Bouldin.

The funeral will be held on Wednesday afternoon at 2 o'clock, with services in Asbury M. E. Church. Interment will be made in Greenmount cemetery. Thomas P. Rice is the funeral director.

William Downs, photographer W.A. Burger, ca. 1885. William Downs was a member of several lodges and was Master Mason of the Fredericktonian Lodge No. 12 during the years 1900-1901 and 1916-1918. In this photo he is wearing an apron and medallion belonging to one of those organizations.

Obituary For William Downs. Reprinted with the permission of the Frederick News-Post and Randall Family, LLC as published in June 1929.

DEATHS.

Wm. H. Downs.

William H. Downs, colored, died at his home, 168 West All Saints street, Sunday morning at 8 45 o'clock, of heart trouble, aged 85 years. He was a member of Fredericktonian Lodge No 12, F. A M., Select Chapter No. 8, R. A M., Hiram Consistory No. 2, 32 degree Masons, Queen Esther Chapter No 2, O. O E. S, Evening Star Pasture No 13, Order of Nazarites, also a member of Asbury M. E church.

He was employed at the Maryland State School for the Deaf for a number of years He is survived by a sister-in-law, Mrs. Alice Bouldin, a niece, Mrs Hettie West, of Frederick, a nephew, Charles Bouldin, of New York City.

Funeral from Asbury M. E. church, Tuesday afternoon at 8 30 o clock Interment in Fairview cemetery A. V. Dixon, funeral director

Obituary for William Downs found in the Frederick Post Archives. June 1929.

Laura Frazier and William Tyler Page circa 1869, Courtesy of the Frederick Historical Society.

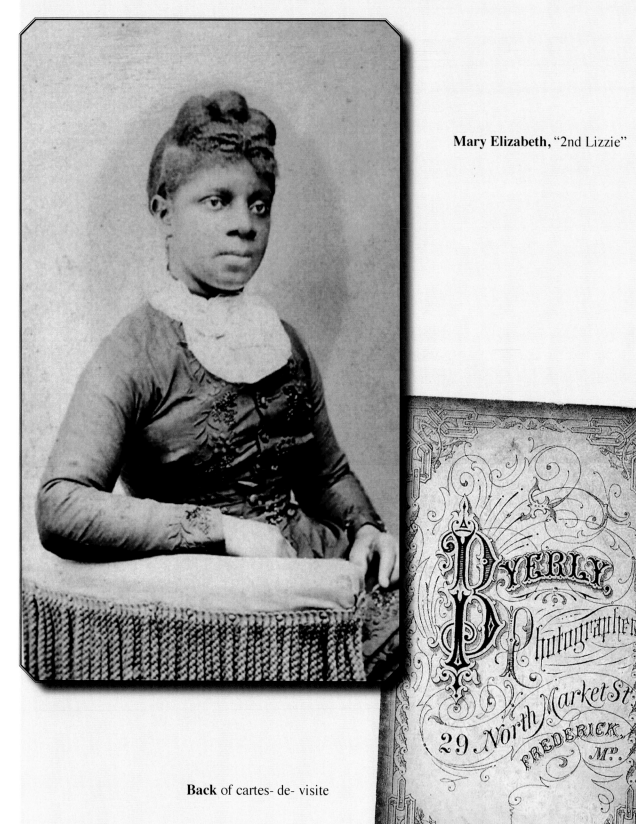

Mary Elizabeth, "2nd Lizzie"

Back of cartes- de- visite

CHAPTER 10

Elizabeth "Second Lizzie" Frazier Oglin

The 2nd Lizzie born Mary Elizabeth on April 18, 1853 survived slavery, but like her brother Charles and sister Martha before her she too died young.

During the early part of 1870 Lizzie lived at the home of her parents while working as a domestic outside the home. Later in that same year seventeen year old Lizzie married a twenty-nine year old widower from Frederick, named Edward Oglin.

By 1871 a child, Mary had been born, and on November 9, 1872 Edward Oglin became a widower for the second time in five years. Mary Elizabeth the 2nd Lizzie was only nineteen years old.

In 1880 Mary was found living with her grandmother, Aunt Laura and cousin Hettie, Edward had married again and was now living outside the city in Pleasantview, Frederick Maryland with his new wife.

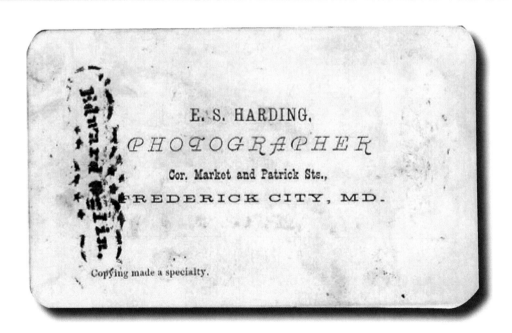

	DATE		PLACE	NAME OF OFFICIAL	TITLE	RESIDENCE OF OFFICIAL		MALE		AGE	COLOR	RESIDENCE	
	Oct	5	1869 St Johns Rectory	Edwd Emma	R.C. Church	Frederick Co. Md.	O'Brien	Dennis		26	White	Washington County	
	Sept	12	1873 Fredk Co. Md.	Wm B. Elzery	Minister		O'Sullivan	Daniel		28	"	Fredrick	Md.
	Feb	18	1879 Johnstup Mill	Eph W. Stoner		Carroll	Ogle	Daniel Alt		26	"	Carroll	
	Oct	14	" Frederick	George Diehl		Fred.	Olm	Daniel		22	"	Fred	"
	Feby	19	1867 Frederick City	Henry C. Elbet	Minister	Frederick Co. Md.	Oglin	Edward		27	Black	Frederick Co. Md.	
	Aug	17	1865	D. Zacharias			Owen	Edward H.		25	White	Montgomery	"
	Aug	31	1870 Co. Md.	J. Nicholson			Oglin	Edward		29	Black	Frederick	
	Feb	23	"	Calvin Ingle			Gould	Elish R.		31	White	New York City N.Y.	
	Oct	22	1872	Joseph Trapnell			Orrison	Edward		32	"	Berkley Co. Va.	
	Feb	12	1873	Danl S. Ferguson			Owings	Elishai T.		40	"	Jefferson Kentucky	
	April	13	1882 City	Irvin D. McCurdy			Oden	Edward		29	"	Fredk Co. Md.	

Back of photo shows a stamped heart enclosed with the name Edward Oglin her father.

RECORD OF MARRIAGES.

Age	Color	Residence	Condition	Occupation	Female	Age	Color	Residence	Condition	Occupation	Date
26	White	Washington County	Single	—	Urilla Matty	19	White	Washington Co. Md	Single		Apl
25	"	Frederick Md	Bachelor	Tinner	Elizabeth McAlister	24	"	Frederick " "	Maid		Sept
26	"	Carroll "		Laborer	Susan Alice Kelly	22	"	" " "			Mar
22	"	Fred "		Farmer	Minnie C. Stull	19	"	" " "			Jan
27	Black	Frederick Co. Md	Single	Laborer	Nancy Fisher	22	Black	Frederick Co. Md	Single		Mar
25	White	Montgomery "		—	Henrietta Brunner	23	White	" " "			Dec
29	Black	Frederick "	Widower	Laborer	May E. Frazier	16	Black	" " "			Apl
31	White	New York City, N.Y.	Bachelor	Physician	Alice R. McLanahan	26	White	" " "			Dec
32	"	Berkley Co. Va.		Railroad	Gertrude Marlow	28	"	" " "			Oct
40	"	Jefferson Kentucky	Widower	Farmer	Marian Nelson	25		" " "	Maid		Mar
29	"	Fredk Co. Md	Bachelor	Laborer	Adda E. Ketty	20	"	" " "			May

Mary Oglin, Photographer E. S. Harding Frederick, Maryland ca 1890

Alice Frazier Bouldin,
Photographer J. Davis Byerly. ca 1880.

CHAPTER 11

Alice Frazier Bouldin

"I dunno how ter read er rite. De white folks didn' 'low us ter l'arn nuthin'. I declar' you bettuh not git kotch wid a papah in you han'. Ef I had half a chance lak you chilluns hab, I'd go ter bed wid mah books."

From interview with Cecelia Chappel, Nashville, Tennessee.
A Folk History of Slavery in the United States, the Federal Writers Project
1936-1938, The Library of Congress.

"I would always go with my mother when she went to Mrs. Alice Frazier Bouldin's home. Mrs. Bouldin had a linen and lace shop on All Saints Street. She loved people and she would always start her conversation with: 'I am Alice Frazier Bouldin. I was born on Record Street. My parents were Millie Butcher, a slave who was married to my father, Charles Frazier, also a slave.'

Mrs. Bouldin, as I remember when I was child of eight years old, had a clear and perfect enunciation of her words. A very short woman in stature, beautiful flawless skin. She was the picture of a strong beautiful God-fearing woman. She was a woman of pride. Her eyes would twinkle when she spoke. She really caught your attention. I shall never forget her. A former slave and a proud woman.

No, I shall never forget Mrs. Alice Frazier Bouldin, as I shall never forget any of the unsung heroes mentioned above.

They all were the STARS of our past. THEY WERE SOMEBODY."

Excerpt of interview with Mrs. Adelaide Dixon Hall,
from the book titled *Memories of Frederick
Over On The Other Side,* by Joy Onley, 1995.

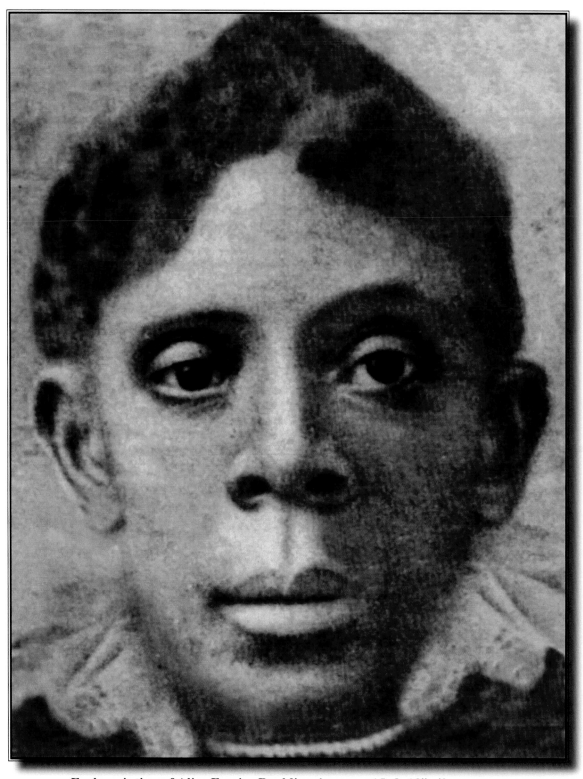

Early painting of Alice Frazier Bouldin, about age 15, 8x10" oil on canvas.
Artist unknown, ca. 1870. According to records kept by the Maryland School For The Deaf in
1868 Alice begun what would become a yearly ritual, assisting at the schools yearly Board of
Visitor meetings. This is what Alice would have looked like during that period.

Cabinet Card of Charles William Bouldin, photographer unknown, ca. 1880. In this photo Charles is dressed in a boy's baby coat, and necktie or bow. He also has on Victorian High Top baby shoes. From the mid 16th century unto the late 19th or early twentieth century young boys in the western world were unbreeched, they wore gowns or dresses. When they turned a certain age they were then dressed in breeches or pants.

**Wallet size profile of
Alice Frazier Bouldin,** ca 1910.

This record of my grandfather and his parents was the first time I had seen the names of either Alice Frazier or George Bouldin. "Saint Street" which probably meant West All Saints Street, during that time and many years to follow was a place where black community, businesses, and culture was vibrant and strong.

En and delivin to Grantee   At the request of George S. Clinton Bopst
        April 26 1904   the following deed is received for record and re-
                              X   corded April 30-1903 at 9½ o'clock A.M.
                                        Test Douglass H. Nargett, Clerk.

This deed made this 22nd day of April in the year nineteen hundred and three by
us, Alice Bouldin and George William Bouldin her husband of New York City
in the State of New York, Witnesseth that in consideration of the Sum of one
thousand dollars we the said Alice Bouldin and George William Bouldin, to
grant unto George S. Clinton Bopst of Frederick City in the State of Maryland, all that lot of ground with the improvements thereon, situated on
the east side of "Public" or "Rineharts" Alley in said City of Frederick
in the State of Maryland and particularly described in a deed from
Peter Frazier and wife and Charles Frazier to Millie Frazier Laura Frazier
and Alice Frazier now the said Alice Bouldin dated the 28th day of April
A.D. 1874 and duly recorded in liber T.G. No. 6 folio 316 one of the land
records of Frederick County, Maryland, the said Millie Frazier who
was the Mother of said Laura Frazier and Alice Frazier, having since
died intestate, leaving the said Laura and Alice as her only heirs
at law and the said Laura, who inter-married with William Downs
having conveyed her undivided one half interest in said lot to the
said Alice Bouldin by deed of the said Laura Downs and William
Downs, her husband, dated the 15 day of October A.D. 1884 and recorded
in liber A.F. No. 9, folio 491, one of the said land records of Frederick
County, as by reference to said deeds will more fully appear.
As to   Witness our hands and seals
Alice Bouldin, test   Alice Bouldin
    John Francis Smith   George William Bouldin   his
State of New York, County, N.Y.   mark
I hereby certify that on this 22 nd day of April in the year nineteen hundred
and three, before me a Notary public of the said State, in and for said

Final sale of property purchased by Peter and Charles Frazier. Alice and husband George Bouldin sold it for one thousand dollars in 1903. The property remained in the family for fifty years. This is also the last documented record found of George Bouldin.

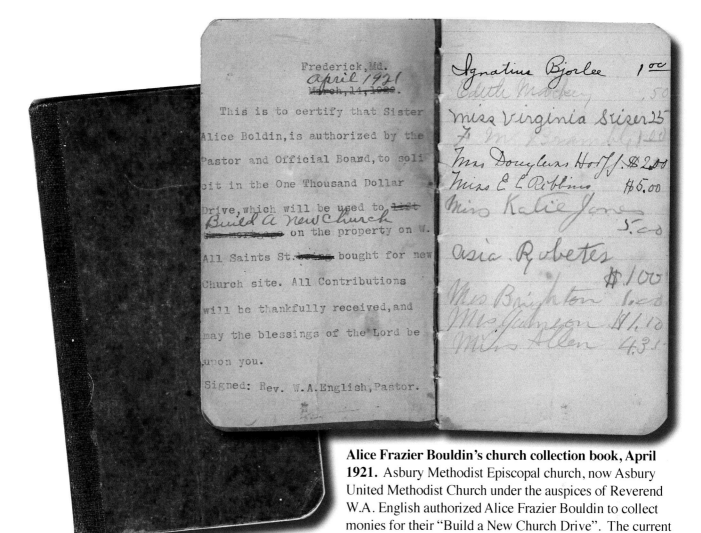

Alice Frazier Bouldin's church collection book, April 1921. Asbury Methodist Episcopal church, now Asbury United Methodist Church under the auspices of Reverend W.A. English authorized Alice Frazier Bouldin to collect monies for their "Build a New Church Drive". The current church building was the result of such fundraising.

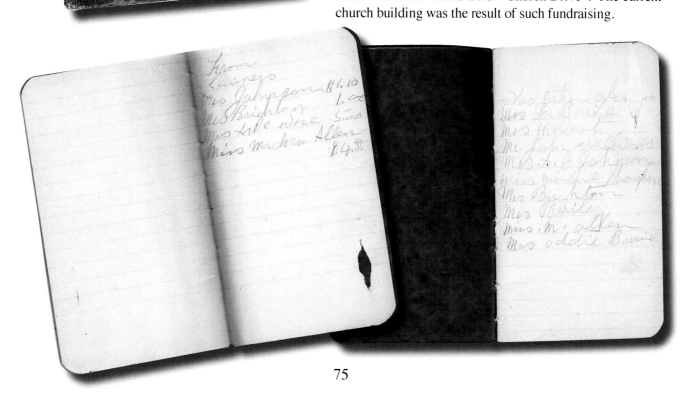

75

Photo Postcard of 1930 Baltimore Washington Annual Conference, Alice Frazier Bouldin wrote on the back of the postcard the conference took place in Westminster, Maryland.

Headshot of Alice Frazier Bouldin.
Such a fancy and stylish hat could usually be seen on the heads of women attending Sunday services or Easter Sunday services, ca. 1920.

Old Main Building, ca 1930.
Alice and William would have worked here. Photo courtesy of the Maryland School For The Deaf.

THE MARYLAND BULLETIN

William Downes and Alice Bouldin. Picture taken in front of Main Building in 1923.

William Downs and Alice Frazier Bouldin appear in a November 1938 issue of the Maryland Bulletin, a publication of The Maryland School For The Deaf. Photo courtesy of the Maryland School For the Deaf.

Mrs. Glidden was pleased with the general appearance of the school and was fascinated by the attractive campus.

The regular monthly visits of Rev. Arthur Bell of New York, on October 9, and Rev. D. E. Moylan, Baltimore, on October 16, took place with the usual classes belonging to the respective denominations, called into session.

Rev. D. E. Moylan, Mr. James Foxwell and Mr. and Mrs. Hansford S. Anderson were with us on November 5. The last named have frequently remembered the library and museum and did not come empty handed this time.

Mr. T. Poole Jones was a recent visitor. As a resident of Frederick, Mr. Jones is deeply interested in the work of the school, an interest which probably developed as a result of his father, Mr. Albert Jones, having been a member of the Board of Visitors of the Maryland School and serving as secretary of the Board from 1911 until the time of his death in 1921.

To many readers of the MARYLAND BULLETIN the picture of William and Alice will bring back memories of by gone years. They saw generations of deaf children come and go. Old William, as he was fondly called, was a bit hazy as to the exact date when he began to serve the school as porter, but Alice remembered distinctly that as a little girl she helped wait on the table at the first dinner served to the Board of Visiors in 1838. She was invited to assist at board meeting time every year until 1935 when frail health prevented her from being on hand. Born in slavery, they spent practically their entire lives in Frederick, and were well known and highly regarded. William continued his services at the school until death terminated his career in June, 1929. Alice passed away last June at the age of 82. Both were prominent in the life of the colored community, William holding various positions in the order of Masonry while Alice was the oldest active member of the Eastern Star.

Wm. Deering & Co. 1888 souvenir advertisement card. Alice was not a farmer, nor was her son. Maybe she knew the proprietor of this business, or just enjoyed the design of the card. Or it is possible that she purchased items from this company for a totally different reason that had nothing to do with farming.

Invite to Grand Supper given by "The Daughters of Conference" at Asbury Church Frederick, Maryland. The Daughters of Conference was begun by Sara Allen in 1827. Mrs. Allen was the second wife of AME Church founder Richard Allen. After witnessing a group of ministers dressed in an unkempt manner at the first annual church conference, Mrs. Allen was inspired to create a women's group which provided food, mended clothing, and supplied support to the ministers.

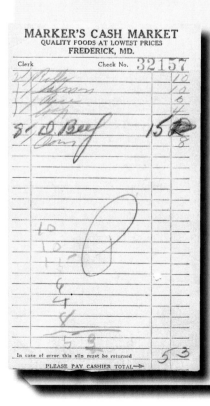

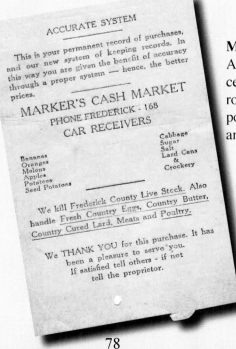

Marker's cash receipt, ca 1930. Alice paid a total of fifty-three cents for what appears to be 2 rolls, some salmon, corn, eight pounds of beef, and four cents for another item.

Asbury Church "Chairman of Auxiliaries" Committee members, part of the 1919 Anniversary Bulletin. The William O. Lee Jr. Collection, Frederick Historical Society. Throughout the years Alice Frazier Bouldin served on many committees including, the Hospitality, Sunday school, and Stewardship.

Sunday Worship. Alice Frazier Bouldin, unidentified gentleman, and woman believed to be Alice's niece Hettie, posed for a photo either before or after church services. Photographer unknown, ca 1930.

Alice Frazier Bouldin often travelled alone to New York to visit friends and family.

Coal receipt for 168 West All Saints Street, 1936. Coal was used to heat homes, operate stoves, and generate hot water.

Household sale: This flyer announces the sale of household items belonging to Alice Frazier Bouldin. Her home was also sold. Doctor Ulysses Grant Bourne, co-founder and president of the Frederick County Branch of the NAACP was the estates executor, and a friend of the family. He stated in court documents that the New York Bouldin's did not wish to hold onto the property located on West All Saints Street because it would be too difficult to maintain from such a distance. In 1919, he and another African American physician, Charles Brooks, opened a hospital at 173 All Saints Street. It operated until 1928. In December 1937 Dr. Bourne took up the issue of equal teacher salaries in Frederick. Initially he tried to negotiate with the Board of Education, but tiring of the Board's tactics in bringing equal pay to black teachers he readied for legal battle and personally offered to finance the case.

Postcard dated March 20, 1930 from F.A. Bernhard & Co. to Alice Frazier Bouldin asking if she would like to place an order for the O.E.S. (Order of Eastern Star), and another organization that is difficult to make out.

Newspaper Clipping from Frederick News Post, 1937. This very interesting clipping torn from a 1937 publication of the Frederick News Post shows a section titled "Fifty and Twenty Years Ago Today in Frederick". Alice only tore out the fifty year portion of the article. The second entry refers to William Tyler Page, grandson to Doctor William Tyler the man who owned Alice Frazier Bouldin, her mother and siblings. Here Alice is clearly documenting her family's connection to the Tyler's albeit his grandson. It is the only physical document found that Alice saved of this sort, maybe there were others, but they are long gone.

The Winter's Farm. In 1889 for reasons unknown thirty-four year old Alice, husband George, and their eleven year old son Charles left Frederick, Maryland and traveled north to the state of New York. Alice stayed in upstate New York for fourteen years, employed as the first colored cook of Bynum Winters.

In 1903 Alice went to live in New York City residing at 989 Fifth Avenue, across from what is now Central Park. Alice did not stay in New York City for very long though, she went back home to Frederick to sell the property her father and uncle had purchased so many years before. When she arrived in Frederick in 1903 she returned alone. Her son Charles, and husband George did not return with her. What happened to Alice and George? She does not mention him in any of her letters. The only time his name was recorded by her was in the Bible where she wrote down their names and her date of marriage.

No photos exist that have been positively identified as George, and there was no notice of death. With the exception of the signed affidavit selling the property on Public Alley in 1903 George seems to have disappeared right after Alice left the Winter Farm.

Census records from 1920 and 1930 list Alice marital status as a widow.

The Winters Farm, Smithboro, N. Y.

Alice Frazier Bouldin learned the importance of documenting and recording important information from her parents. Here she adds a second and third generation to the small book began by them.

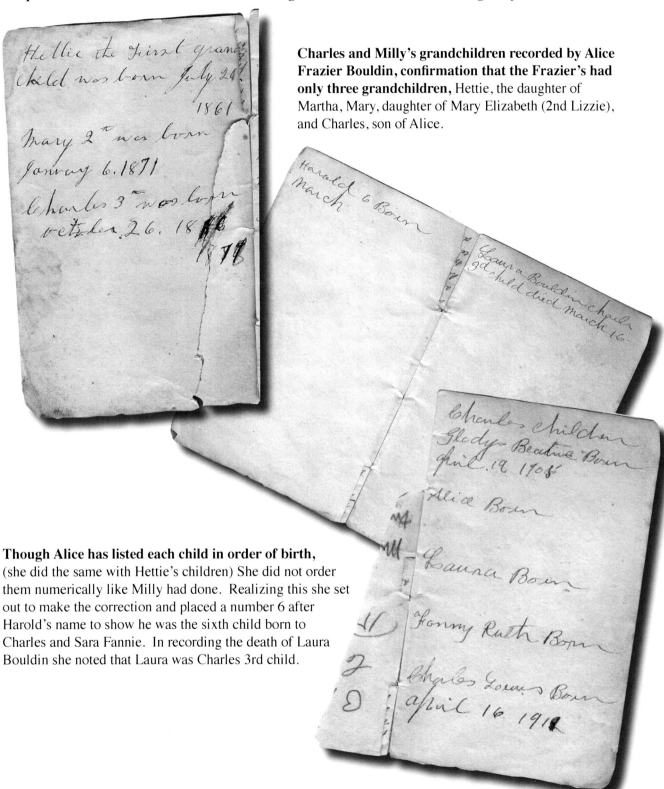

Charles and Milly's grandchildren recorded by Alice Frazier Bouldin, confirmation that the Frazier's had only three grandchildren, Hettie, the daughter of Martha, Mary, daughter of Mary Elizabeth (2nd Lizzie), and Charles, son of Alice.

Though Alice has listed each child in order of birth, (she did the same with Hettie's children) She did not order them numerically like Milly had done. Realizing this she set out to make the correction and placed a number 6 after Harold's name to show he was the sixth child born to Charles and Sara Fannie. In recording the death of Laura Bouldin she noted that Laura was Charles 3rd child.

President Lincoln greets a young Alice Frazier on Record Street, October 1862. Illustration by Danielle E. West.

Wednesday, February 19, 1957

LINCOLN TOPIC BEFORE CLUB

Judge Edward S. Delaplaine Addresses Welcome Wagon Newcomers

An affidavit made 22 years ago by a Frederick woman that she was greeted by Abraham Lincoln in Frederick when he was on his way from Antietam to Washington, was one of the "sidelights" given by Judge Edward S. Delaplaine yesterday before the Welcome Wagon Newcomers Club in the Francis Scott Key Hotel.

The speaker said that he prepared the affidavit for Alice Bouldin, colored, at the request of Mrs. Francis H. Markell, D. A. R. regeat. It was made before F. Ross Myers, notary public.

According to the affidavit, Mrs. Bouldin's mother worked for Dr. William Tyler, one of Frederick's leading physicians and president of the Farmers and Mechanics National Bank. Dr. Tyler lived on Record street in the house marked by the D. A. R. as the birthplace of his grandson, William Tyler Page, author of the American Creed.

Lincoln stopped at the home of Mrs. James M. Ramsey, one of Dr. Tyler's daughters, also on Record street, now the home of Commander and Mrs. Dudley Page. General Hartsuff was nursed there after being wounded at Antietam. Judge Delaplaine said he supposed that Dr. Tyler attended the general.

Mrs. Bouldin swore that Lincoln noticed her, then 10 years old, and asked her what her name was and gave her some money.

Visits General Greely

Judge Delaplaine gave a description of Winfield Scott Schley's rescue of Adolphus W. Greely and six companions in the Arctic in 1884, and told of his own visit with Greely when the explorer was 91 years old.

AFFIDAVIT OF ALICE BOULDIN REGARDING

THE VISIT OF ABRAHAM LINCOLN IN FREDERICK,

MARYLAND

I, Alice Bouldin, of Frederick, Maryland, will
be eighty years old in October, 1934.

My mother, Milly Butcher, once a slave, married Charles
Frazier, also a slave; my mother belonged to Dr. William Tyler, who lived
in the house now owned by Mr. William Crawford Johnson, in which house
I was born.

Before coming to Frederick
My mother/belonged to Mrs. Rice of Libertytown, Mary
land; my father to Mr. James Coale of the same place.

After the Battle of Gettysburg, President Lincoln
came to Frederick to visit General Shires, who was Wounded at the Battle
of Gettysburg and was taken to the home of Mrs. Nelly Ramsey, a daughter
of Dr. William Tyler.

Mr. Lincoln arrived for a noon dinner, which was served
by the old family slaves; and I, a child of ten years, passing back and
forth attracted the attention of the President, who asked my name. I told
him my name was Alice Frazier, and he gave me a paper bill of the value
of five cents. The cook, Caroline Charlton, told me to take the paper
bill to Bopst's store to buy her five cents worth of Rapoe's snuff.

At the dinner were present Mrs. Ramsey and her husband,
Col. James Ramsey, and Miss Susie Ramsey and Miss Nellie Ramsey, also
Miss Nannie Tyler (Mrs. Walker Y. Page, the mother of Mr. Wm. Tyler
Page).

This occurred in the home now owned by Mr. and

Affidavit of Alice Frazier Bouldin regarding the visit of Abraham Lincoln to Frederick, Maryland.

(#2.)

Mrs. Dudley Page, Record Street, Frederick, Maryland.

After dinner Mr. Lincoln shook with all the members of the family and all the slaves and then left for Washington.

Alice Bauldin

STATE OF MARYLAND,

FREDERICK COUNTY, SCT:

I hereby certify that on this 28th day of May, in the year 1936, before me, the subscriber, a Notary Public of the state of Maryland, in and for Frederick County aforesaid, personally appeared Alice Bouldin, of Frederick, Maryland, and made oath in due form of law that the matters and things stated in the aforegoing statement are true to the best of ~~my~~/her knowledge and belief.

In testimony whereof, witness my hand and notarial seal on the ~~date~~/last above written. _Alice Bauldin_

F. Ross Myers

NOTARY PUBLIC.

Letter dated March 7, 1920 from Alice Frazier Bouldin to her granddaughter Alice Bouldin. Transcribed: My Dear granddaughter a few lines to let you know how glad I was to get your nice letter. I hope you will write often for I always want to hear from you all. I think of you all so often and am glad whenever you write to me. I hope the children will get over this cold winter alright. I have just written to your father to thank him for the World Almanac he sent to Uncle Billie. I had a letter from Mrs. Richardson and she was asking me how you was she said she would like to hear from you. Why don't you write to her- her address Mrs. Florence Richardson 601 Union St Hudson New York. You did not tell me what kind of work you are doing I am glad that you and Gladys are working and I hope you both are good enough to help your mother and father this cold weather I will be glad when I get the pictures I hope you are a good girl and mind what Mrs. Daisy and Mrs. Lizzie tells - Hettie and Arie and the Boys all send love to you all. I am glad you go over to see the folks in Yonkers, now be a good girl I want you and Gladys to come to Frederick to see all of us next summer. Now remember me to Mrs. Daisy and Mrs. Lizzie and the folks at home - also Mrs. Frazier and Johnny and family write soon to you. Grandmother Alice Bouldin.

Alice Frazier Bouldin was sixty-five years of age at the time this letter was written, her granddaughter Alice Bouldin was fifteen. In the letter Alice refers to her two granddaughters using the term girl or girls, and Hettie's four sons John, Thomas, Franklin, and Marshall as "Boys", even though all are well into their teens or young men and women by this time. When mentioning children not in their teens she calls them children, line 3. The children she's referring to are the six younger siblings of Alice and Gladys who range in ages from one to twelve years of age. On line four she speaks about writing her son and thanking him for the world almanac, the Uncle Billie she is talking about is William Downs. On line 10 she makes reference to Alice visiting Yonkers, Charles, and his wife lived in Yonkers before moving down to the city. The connection between family and extended family is clearly evident in this letter. As well as the expectation that children are to be respectful and helpful to their parents. Alice Frazier Bouldin's influence on the lives of her grandchildren was clear as she reminds and encourages her granddaughter to write, visit, and mind other adults who may not be family but should be treated as so. She also acknowledges her granddaughters as young adults by complimenting their employment and she further inquires about the type of work they are doing. This letter gives insight into the relationships Alice Frazier Bouldin had with her own parents, siblings, son, and larger community, as well as the complexity of those hierarchies.

Alice and Gladys Bouldin, photographer unknown, ca. 1906. Alice Frazier Bouldin must have been beside herself at the births of her first grandchildren. The back of the photo says that it was addressed to Hettie in Frederick, Maryland, whether it ever made it to Hettie or was retrieved once Hettie died in 1935 is unclear.

Gladys Bouldin and Grandmother Alice Frazier Bouldin in backyard of Alice's home on West All Saints Street, ca 1937.

Left to right: Alice Bouldin in doorway of 168 West All Saints, Alice and Grandmother Alice Frazier Bouldin, Gladys Bouldin in front of car.

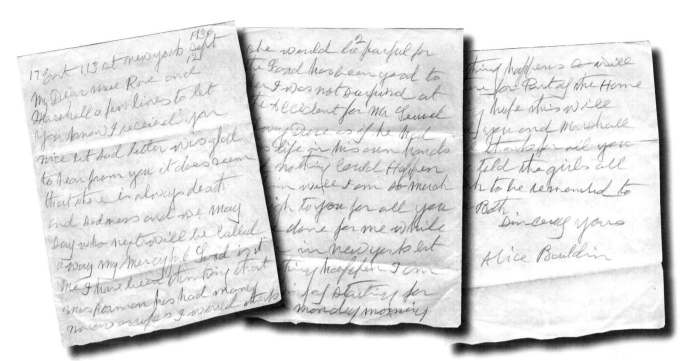

Letter from Alice Frazier Bouldin to Mae Rose and Marshall September 12, 1936.

17 East 113th Street, New York, Sept 12 1936

My Dear Mae Rose and Marshall just a few lines to let you know I received your nice but sad letter was glad to hear from you it does seem that there is always death and sadness and so we may say who next will be called away my merciful Lord is it me I have been thinking about Mrs. Forman she's had many narrow escapes I would think she would be fearful as the Lord has been good to her - I was not surprised by the accident for Mr. Sewell always Dare as if he had his life in his own hands and nothing could happen to him will I am so much obliged to you for all you have done for me while I am in New York If nothing happens I am thinking of starting for home Monday morning if nothing happens so will be there for part of the homecoming Hope this will find you and Marshall well thanks for all you have told the girls wish to be remembered to you both.   Sincerely Yours, Alice Bouldin

Written in 1936, Alice Bouldin Frazier was eighty-two years of age. The Marshall this letter is addressed to is Hettie's youngest son, and his wife at the time, Mae Rose (they divorced some time later and she remarried). In this letter it is difficult not to hear and feel Alice's strength and faith in God. If one did not know of her commitment to her faith it would almost appear as if she lacked empathy for the two individuals mentioned in the letter. The Mr. Sewell she speaks about was a dear friend of her for many years, they served on several church committees together and found in her papers was his obituary torn from the Frederick Post News, it states Mr. Sewell died February 8, 1937, this was shortly after his accident and the writing of this letter. The address at the top of the letter shows that Alice was in the home of her son and children. The homecoming Alice writes about is most likely a reference to Mrs. Forman's funeral- "she is going home to the Lord".

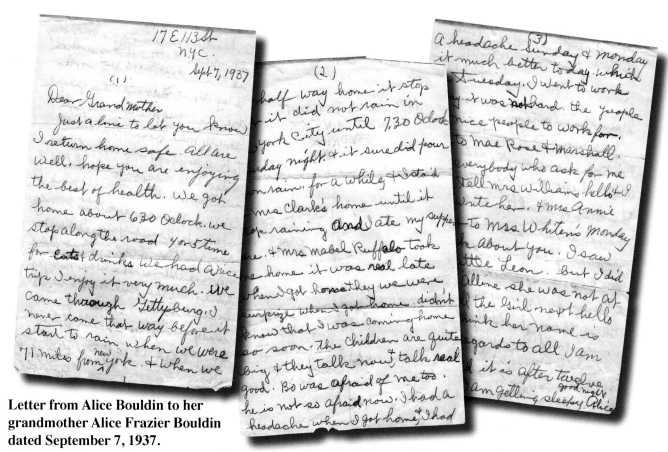

Letter from Alice Bouldin to her grandmother Alice Frazier Bouldin dated September 7, 1937.

Alice Bouldin was thirty-two years old and Alice Frazier Bouldin was eighty-two.

17 E. 113th St. N.Y.C. Sept 7, 1937

Dear Grandmother

Just a line to let you know I return home safe. All are well. I hope you are enjoying the best of health. We got home around 6.30 o clock. We stop along the road 4 or 5 time for eats and drinks, we had a nice trip I enjoy it very much. We came through Gettysburg I never came that way before. It start to rain when we were 71 miles from New York & we got half way home & it stop but it did not rain in New York City until 7.30 o clock Saturday night and it sure did pour down rain for a while, & I staid at Mrs. Clark's home until it stopped raining & I ate my supper there and Mrs. Mabel Ruffalo took me home it was real late when I got home they were surprised when I got home didn't know I was coming home so soon the children are quite big & they talk now & talk real good. Bo was afraid of me too. He is not so afraid now I had a headache when I got home & I had a headache Sunday & Monday it much better today which is Tuesday I went to work today it was not hard. The people are nice people to work for. Love to Mae Rose & Marshall. Tell everyone who ask for me hello. Tell Mrs. Williams hello & I will write her & Mrs. Annie. I Went to Mrs. Whiten's Monday she ask about you I saw big & little Leon but I did not see Alline she was not at home. Tell the girl next hello for me I think her name is Gladys regards to all I am going to bed it is after twelve o clock & I am getting sleepy.   Good Night, Alice

Alice is returning home to New York City from somewhere south, she said that she came through Gettysburg so she may have been in Frederick, traveling north through Pennsylvania, and Upstate New York. The children Alice Bouldin mentions are her nieces and nephews, Alice Frazier Bouldin's great grandchildren. At the time of this letter there were 6 great grandchildren: Gloria, Charlotte, Raymond, Geraldine, Harold, and Walter (Bo). Alice tells her grandmother she has gone back to work after a long weekend of travel. She says she is ok with her job and that the people were nice people to work for, this implies that she was working in the home of someone. Domestic jobs- maids, servants, cooks, nannies, washwoman, were often the only employment uneducated and often educated black women could get to support themselves and their families.

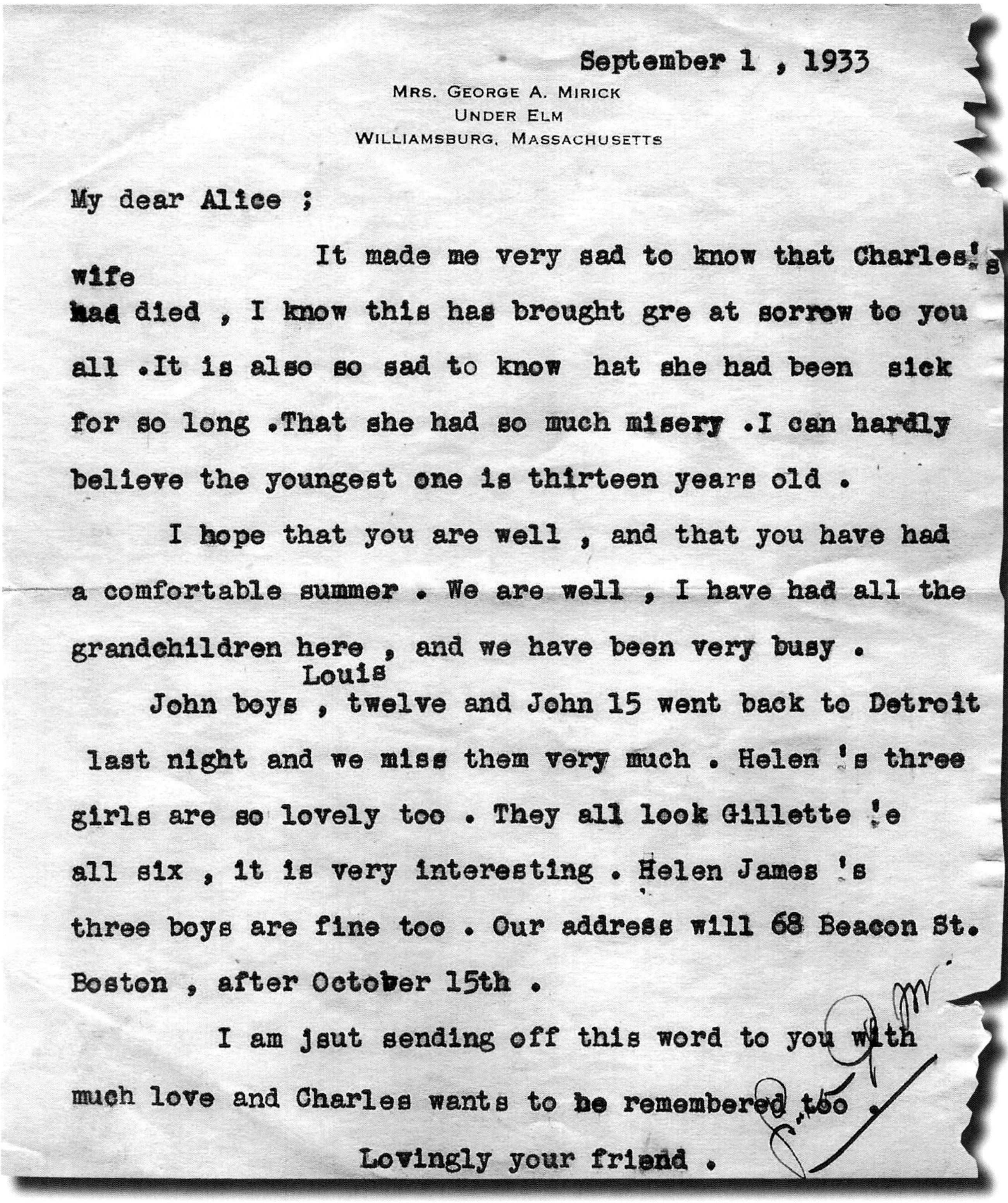

September 1 , 1933

MRS. GEORGE A. MIRICK
UNDER ELM
WILLIAMSBURG, MASSACHUSETTS

My dear Alice ;

wife
          It made me very sad to know that Charles's
had died , I know this has brought gre at sorrow to you
all .It is also so sad to know hat she had been   sick
for so long .That she had so much misery .I can hardly
believe the youngest one is thirteen years old .

     I hope that you are well , and that you have had
a comfortable summer . We are well , I have had all the
grandchildren here , and we have been very busy .
              Louis
John boys , twelve and John 15 went back to Detroit
last night and we miss them very much . Helen 's three
girls are so lovely too . They all look Gillette 'e
all six , it is very interesting . Helen James 's
three boys are fine too . Our address will 68 Beacon St.
Boston , after October 15th .

     I am jsut sending off this word to you with
much love and Charles wants to be remembered too .
           Lovingly your friend .

Letter from Mrs. George Mirick to Alice Frazier Bouldin dated September 1933 regarding the death of her daughter-in-law Sara Fanny Bouldin.

Death Announcement and Obituary of Alice Frazier Bouldin, who died June 7, 1938 she was eighty-two years old.

MRS. ALICE FRASHER BOULDINN

who is a member of Asbury M. E. Church, was born at 109 Record Street, Frederick, Maryland October 27, 1855. She joined Asbury Church in 1870 at the age of 15 years.

She remembers the first Negro pastor of Asbury Church, who was Rev. R. H. Robinson, in 1864.

She was present at the organization of the Church School in Sharp Street Church January, 1869; 69 years ago. She has the letter she wrote her father telling him of that organization.

She shook hands with Abraham Lincoln on Record Street in Frederick in 1865 when he was on his way to Gettysburg, Pennsylvania from Washington. He gave her five cents in brown paper money.

She remembers a great deal about the Washington Conference from the time it was organized.

She attends church almost every Sunday morning, she attends both services some Sundays. She walks anywhere she wants over town, does her own house work, hears well; writes letters and makes her own clothes. She went to New York alone last year to visit her son and grandchildren.

She is a very pleasant and kind person. We all love her.

The funeral of Mrs. Alice Frasher Bouldin, colored, took place from Asbury M. E. church Friday afternoon at 2:30 o'clock, with services conducted by Rev. E. E. Williams, assisted by Rev. H. L. McClendon, Rev. J. M. Beane, Rev. J. C. Norris, Rev. C. E. Hodgis, Rev. R. E. Burnette. A solo, "In The Land Where You Never Grow Old" was sung by Mrs. Helen Correy. Pallbearers were Richard Walker, William Rollins, Samuel Stroud, Thomas Strother, William Roberts, Livious Stanton. The deceased was a member of Eastern Star No. 2 for 60 years. Interment Fairview cemetery. M. R. Etchison and Son, funeral directors.

PERSONALS

Powell and Hinsugh, funeral directors.

MRS. ALICE F. BOULDIN.

The funeral of Mrs. Alice Frasher Bouldin, colored, who died at the age of 82 years at her home, 168 West All Saints street, Tuesday evening, will take place at 2:30 o'clock this afternoon at the Asbury Methodist Episcopal church. Until one o'clock on Friday the body will rest at the late residence. Interment will be in the Fairview cemetery. M. R. Etchison and Son, funeral directors.

SICK

In September 2006 my cousins Alyce Baker, James Tilmon, and I traveled to Fairview Cemetery in Frederick, Maryland determined to locate Alice Frazier Bouldin's gravesite. I had been to the cemetery on two previous occasions but was unsuccessful in my search. We arrived at the cemetery just before dusk, and were greeted by the care taker, Mr. Bernard Brown who had bought along the cemetery's ledger to help with our search.

Mr. Brown directed us to an area of the cemetery where Alice might have been buried. Finding no marker or headstone we began to look through the cemetery's ledger. After a few minutes of what we all agreed was a thorough search, we closed the book and began to look at the site again. Mr. Brown said that he was sure he could find something since that area is where he had buried a vault previously. As the last rays of sun began to fade we headed back to our cars, quiet in our own thoughts and disappointed that again we were not able to find Alice. Before anyone could enter their cars Mr. Brown suggested we take one last look through the cemetery's ledger. This time when the pages were turned

the Bouldin name in bright red ink seem to jump out at us. As we scanned the page with our eyes we were stunned to find the names of Charles Frazier, his wife Milly Butcher Frazier, Peter and Hannah Frazier, and Laura Frazier Downs, all of whom had been reburied in Fairview from their original burial site in Greenmount Cemetery. Underneath those entries were William Downs, husband of Laura, and Alice Frazier Bouldin.

Several months later in November 2006, I received a letter from Mr. Brown. He had returned to the cemetery to place a marker at the location where our ancestors had been buried when he decided to check if there were any stones buried in the ground underneath. The ledger mentioned seven people but there were no visible stones for any of them. Amazingly two headstones were unearthed that had been buried for years, they were those of Charles and Milly Frazier. In June 2007, nearly seventy years to the day of Alice Frazier Bouldin's passing a stone was placed to memorialize those ancestors whose resting place was lost but then found.

93

THESE CHAINS, O BROTHERS MINE,
HAVE WEIGHED US DOWN

AS SAMSON
IN THE TEMPLE OF THE GODS;

UNLOOSEN THEM
AND LET US BREATHE THE AIR

THAT MAKES THE GOLDENROD
THE FLOWER OF CHRIST.

Fenton Johnson
1888-1958

CHAPTER 12

Charles & Sara Frances Bouldin

Charles William Bouldin was born October 26, 1878 in Frederick, Maryland the only child of Alice Frazier and George William Bouldin. Charles left Frederick in 1889 with his parents, and though his mother returned to Maryland he did not. Charles was not a tall man. He was just under five feet seven inches, with a slight built, and his mother's slender face. Charles and his mother Alice shared a very close relationship they kept in touch through letters, photographs, and frequent visits back and forth between Maryland and New York City. On December 12, 1903 he married sixteen year old Sarah Frances (also known as Sara Fannie) Qualls of Manhattan. Soon the Bouldin's would welcome into the world their first child, daughter Gladys. In all Charles and Sara Fannie would have eleven children, Gladys, Mary Alice, Laura, Fanny Ruth, Charles Lewis (my father), Harold George, Dorothy Irene, Kenneth William, Ida May, Harriet (Hattie) Marie, and Shirley, they were the fourth generation of Frazier's- who now called their home New York. In 1920 a census record for Yonkers, New York list both Charles and Sara Fannie as employed, he as a Milner or hat maker, and she a Tailor. This was also the year Hattie was born and when they would leave the outskirts of New York State for the city of Manhattan for good.

In June 1933 Sara Fannie died in Bellevue Hospital after a long illness, she was forty-seven years old. Her two youngest daughters Ida May and Hattie were fourteen and thirteen. Papa like his grand-parents Charles and Milly did whatever was necessary and kept his family together. Each child it was said had nothing but kind and generous words for this man who devoted himself to his family.

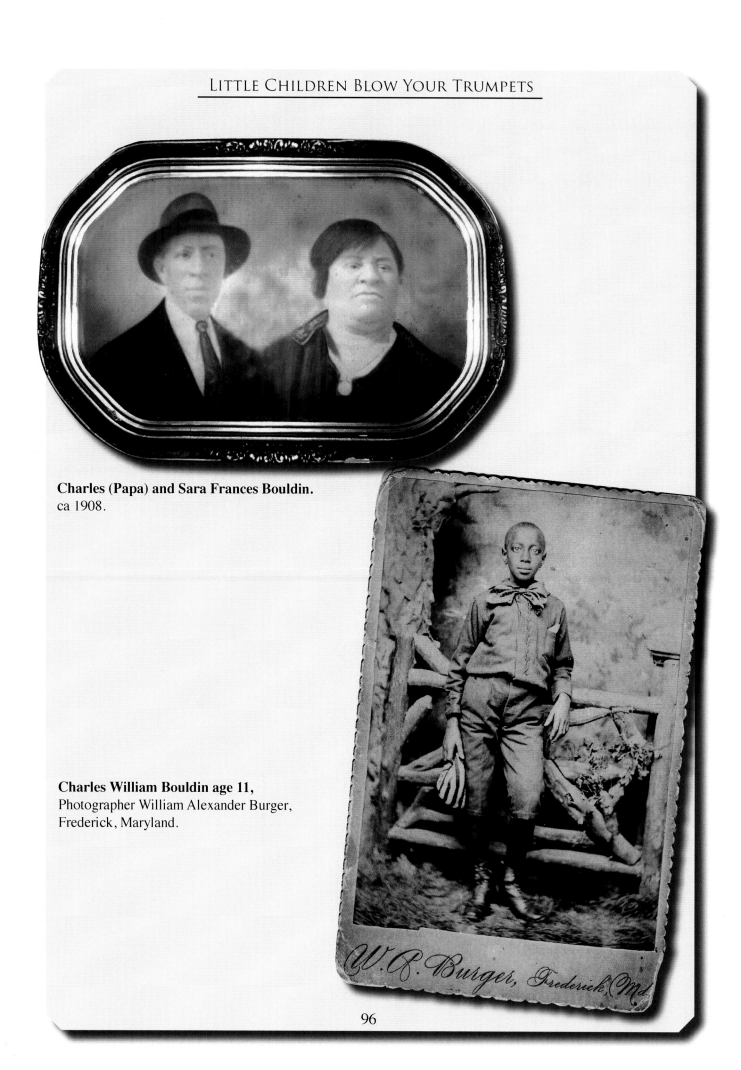

Charles (Papa) and Sara Frances Bouldin.
ca 1908.

Charles William Bouldin age 11,
Photographer William Alexander Burger,
Frederick, Maryland.

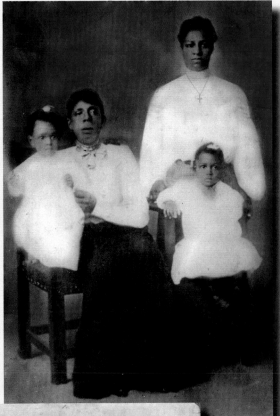

Family portrait, ca. 1906, New York. Seated Alice Frazier Bouldin holding granddaughter Alice Bouldin age fourteen months. Standing: daughter –in-law Sara Fannie, seated in front of her mother is Gladys Bouldin age two.

Gladys Bouldin, 1907, age three years seven months.

Wilhemenia Willis ca. 1907 was the daughter of Martha Fernidad older sister of Sara Fannie. Wilhemenia was raised in the home of her aunt and uncle from a young age. In 1920 a census record lists Wilhemenia as a daughter of Charles and Sara Fannie.

Harlem, New York, ca. 1913, Sara Fannie seated with daughter Dorothy, age one, Charles standing, daughter Fanny Ruth age four. Photos that were taken on the rooftops of tenements in New York City during this period were possibly due to the crowded streets below.

Card Cabinet photo of Sara Fannie, ca. 1908.

Charles Bouldin, Harlem, New York, ca 1920's.

My dearest friend
on earth besides
mother is
"Fanny"

Fanny Ruth with friend could also be one
of her sisters, ca. 1927.

Back of photo

Mother's Day
I gladly pay you tribute
Since you have proved to be
The very best of Mother's
In all the world --- to me.

Mother's day card from Gladys Bouldin
to her mother Sara Fannie, ca. 1916.

99

Charles Bouldin, August 4, 1969, sitting on the stoop of 1178 Bushwick Avenue.

Postcard from Charles Bouldin to his daughter Ida Baker, July 1949. Charles maintained relationships with family and friends in Frederick years after the death of his mother. The last year of his life, suffering from senility, Charles made several trips alone to Frederick. The family, though worried always knew where to find Papa. It is believed that he boarded the train, a route that he and his mother had travelled so many times before.

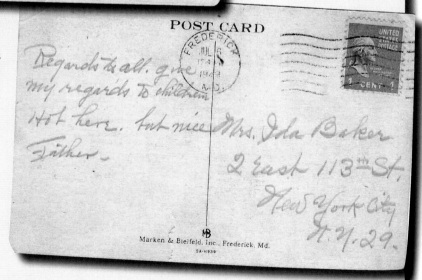

Charles Bouldin (Papa) cuts into cake celebrating his 76th birthday. Charles died at the age of 94 in 1972. Charles Bouldin was affectionately called Papa by his children, grandchildren and great grandchildren.

Envelope addressed to Charles Bouldin from someone in Frederick, May 1906. The letter removed from the envelope was not found.

Easter Sunday 1930, Charles Bouldin.

Photo believed to be that of Thomas Williams's son of Hettie Frazier Williams West and grandson of Martha Frazier. Thomas served in World War I.

Thomas Williams Draft Registration Card dated June 5, 1918. The United States drafted four million young men by the summer of 1918.

Either Thomas never married or was widowed by the year 1944. He lists Doctor U. G. Bourne as both his employer and contact person on this registration card.

Thomas E. Williams, Fairview Cemetery, Frederick, Maryland. I stumbled upon this headstone while searching for Alice Frazier Bouldin's. He is buried several feet from his great grandparents Charles and Milly.

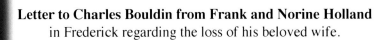

Frederick, Md.,
June, 10th '33

#1706 - Park Ave.,
New York City,

Dear Charles;—

I have just learned with deep sorrow and much regret that you have lost your dear good wife, and it certainly pains me, that it is impossible for me to be with you personally, and I know full well how futile it is to address and worry you with mere idle words in this hour of anguish and sorrow, with which it has pleased God to visit you and take away your dear helpmate, and shall not say more than to tell you the loss of her, is a deep sorrow to me and my wife.

We beg to remain yours;

In deep sympathy and affection,

Frank & Norine Holland

Letter to Charles Bouldin from Frank and Norine Holland
in Frederick regarding the loss of his beloved wife.

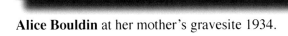

Alice Bouldin at her mother's gravesite 1934.

After the death of Sara Frances in 1933, Charles was left to raise his children on his own.
Charles (Papa) so loved his wife that on Memorial Day of each year he summoned his children and
grandchildren to her gravesite, where they gathered in celebration of her life. When Papa died in 1972,
my father Pike arranged for us to attend the funeral. I can still recall the ride from our home in the South
Bronx to Bushwick, Brooklyn, in one of my father's old station wagons. Though we were quite young
at the time, the significance of the occasion did not escape my sister and I. We have often discussed that
day and the homecoming we witnessed, a man of great honor had passed on and he was our grandfather.

**Charles Bouldin with two
of his three sons,** from left
to right: Charles (Pike),
Charles (Papa), and
Kenneth. Ca. 1950.

Gladys, Ida, Papa, Dorothy, and Alice, ca 1950.

Charles with four of his granddaughters, ca 1954, left to right: standing, Barbara, Papa, and Loretta, kneeling left to right: Frances and Alyce.

Papa surrounded by several of his children, and grandchildren, ca. 1950.

Charles William Bouldin and Alice Frazier Bouldin. There was no one to ask who had placed these two photos together in this frame. The shading underneath each picture, and the receipt for the frame remain they give a clue that these photos were placed together many years before. No pictures have been found of mother and son taken together. These framed photos may well be a substitute for that photo.

CHAPTER 13

Grandchildren & Great Grandchildren of Alice Frazier Bouldin

Of the eleven documented Bouldin births nine would live to adulthood, six girls and three boys. They were: Gladys, Alice, Fanny, Dorothy, Ida, Harriet, Charles, Harold, and Kenneth. With the exception of Kenneth, all lived long lives into their seventies, eighties, and nineties. By the year 1920 the entire family had settled into Harlem, New York. The siblings were very close, at one point after the death of their mother in 1933, most could be found residing at 113 W. 117th Street. From 1986-1995 at least two Bouldin children shared the residences in Bushwick, Brooklyn. City life from the early nineteen twenties on was becoming increasingly difficult Blacks, unemployment was high, and Jim Crow Laws intended to discriminate against blacks were proving quite successful. However, regardless of these injustices the Bouldin's like thousands of their people continued on. They traveled out of state, attended school, celebrated graduations, communions, birthdays, and births. Much like the Frazier's they enjoyed being photographed, and took casual photos of everyday life as well as professional studio photos. Several photos found were taken by the renowned African American photographer James Van Der Zee, and just like the Frazier's they believed in looking sharp for the occasion. All were employed and believed in an honest day's work. While several completed secondary school most left right after the primary grades. (This was not unusual for the time period often children/teens went to work to help support the family). Both Gladys and Alice worked as domestics from an early age. Alice would later do factory work for a blouse company in Queens. Ida May and Dorothy also did factory work or piece work as it was called. Fanny Ruth worked in a dress boutique somewhere in Manhattan as early as 1930. Pike held various jobs. In his teens he was employed at a slaughterhouse, later he cleared and cleaned buildings for future renovation, moved furniture, and later became a long distance trucker. Kenneth and Harold were both World War II Veterans. Kenneth was a machinist during and after the war. In 1926 the first great grandchild was born. She was named Gloria, the daughter of Fanny Ruth. Next followed Charlotte Baker in 1929, she was the daughter of Dorothy.

Eighteen great grandchildren were born between the years 1926 and 1965; sadly half would precede their parents in death, but not before starting families of their own.

Left to right Kenneth, Harriet (Hattie), Ida May Bouldin, Christmas 1924, Harlem, New York.

Siblings Kenneth and Alice holding unidentified toddler on roof top, ca. 1930.

Sisters Dorothy and Alice Bouldin ca. 1928.

109

Class pictures of Ida May Bouldin, and Harriet Bouldin. Public School 86 was located on Lexington Avenue and 96th Street in Manhattan during the 1930's. The school was listed in The World's Almanac and Facts for New York City in 1898, making it over thirty years old at the time of these photos and possibly much older. This would account for the worn out appearance of the classrooms in each photo. The school building is no longer located on 96th and Lexington.

Ida May Bouldin, ca. 1928, second student from the left standing.

Harriet Bouldin ca. 1930, sixth student from the left.

THE 3RD. YEAR INTERMEDIATE CLASS. S. S.

Miss Mary Hazel, Supt. Intermediate Dept. There are in all departments of the Sunday School 115. Mrs. J. C. Walker is Supt. of the Cradle Roll. Mrs. J. R. Tucker of the Home Dept. We are expecting to have our first graduates from our training department this year.

This advertisement from Hudson, New York shows a class of students from a third year intermediate class for a Sunday school. Students were possibly being trained as seamstress, typist, woodworkers or metal workers. Gladys Bouldin is standing on left wearing hat, ca. 1920.

Charles Lewis Bouldin, (Pike) age 23, 1933.

PFC Harold Bouldin
November 3, 1943, Chillicothe, Ohio.

Kenneth Bouldin, the caption on the back
of the photo reads, "Somewhere in France
December 1944.

Alice Bouldin, ca. 1937, Alice Bouldin never married or had children.
She died in 1987, she was eighty-two.

Fanny Ruth, ca. 1924

Alice Bouldin and two friends, on rooftop of Harlem Building, ca. 1940.

Ida May Bouldin Baker, April 4, 1944, N.Y.C.

Harriet Marie Bouldin Daniels, (called Hattie) last of the Bouldin's nine children, born in 1920, ca. 1945, she married twice and had three children, Charles Lewis Baker, Richard Daniels and Dorothy Gloria Daniels.

Dorothy and Charlotte on rooftop. Ca. 1944

Charles Lewis Bouldin (Pike)

My family Portrait in 1968, my mother Diana Washington, top row left to right: Keith, Michael. 2nd row: Charles, Tanya, Terrance and Patricia.

Tanya Washington, 1966

Patricia Washington, 1966

Dorothy Bouldin Black, ca. 1940.

Gladys Bouldin ca. 1908.

FOR WE HAVE BEEN WITH THEE
IN NO MAN'S LAND,

THROUGH LAKE OF FIRE
AND DOWN TO HELL ITSELF;

AND NOW WE ASK OF THEE OUR LIBERTY,
OUR FREEDOM
IN THE LAND OF STARS AND STRIPES.

I AM GLAD THAT THE PRINCE OF PEACE
IS HOVERING OVER NO MAN'S LAND.

Fenton Johnson
1888-1958

LOOKING FOR YOUR ANCESTORS

TIPS TO BEGIN
LOOKING FOR YOUR ANCESTORS

PHOTOS

Try to gather as many photos as you can. Use the 5 W's to assist you. Who is in the photo? Or What is in the Photo? Who gave you the photo? What was going on in the photo? What type of clothing were the subjects wearing? What is the subject about? Where was the photo taken? Why and when was the photo taken? The style of dress of the subject and landmarks appearing in the photo can help you date it. Also try to identify the name of the photographer or studio where the photo was taken. The photographer's information can help you date your photo and may also provide you with information about family traditions, activities, practices, social and economic status, employment, and what was going on in the life of the person at the time of the photo. Do not just rely on photos already in your family. Historical Societies, Churches, and Newspapers, and magazine articles, Flea Markets, Thrift Stores, and Antiques Shops may also have photos related to your area or research. School year books are also a good source of information, imagine finding a school yearbook with a photo of your grandparents during their adolescence years.

FAMILY HISTORY

Ask questions, be a busy body. Contact your family's historian (the person who keeps in touch with everyone, organizes the family reunion, creates and updates family trees and who may have documented histories of your family both oral and written). If you are researching family who were slaves search the principal family information (slave owners), as if you were researching your own family. Family letters, old bills, insurance policies, receipts, subscriptions, train schedules, flyers, they all mean something and can tell you a lot about a person's life.

CENSUS RECORDS

Online and hardcopies (hardcopies can be found in the state or national archives, historical societies, and libraries. Hardcopies are different from online resources and microfilm; hardcopies of census records are found in a book. The census records which appear on pages 3 and 4 12 were found in a genealogy book. Don't let spellings, or shortened names throw you for a loop, when researching the census records it is a good idea to search the Soundex records, Soundex is based on the sounds of the surnames and not the spelling. I was two years into my research when I figured out that the Amelia listed in an 1880 census was actually my 2nd great-grandmother Milly. Every document I came upon listed her name as Milly, even her tombstone had the name Milly on it, but I did not make the connection early on. But because there were some familiar names listed in the household on that 1880 census record, I recorded the information in my journal and was able to go back to it at a later date when I realized Amelia and Milly were the same person.

CEMETERIES

I suggest visiting the cemetery you believe your subjects are in if possible. If this is not an option try contacting and the caretaker who will have access to the cemetery ledger. The ledger will tell you if your ancestor is buried in that particular cemetery. I had not been successful in locating Alice's gravesite in the cemetery even though I had information from her obituary that she was buried in there. However with the assistance of the caretaker and the cemetery ledger we found Alice, her parents Charles and Milly, uncle Peter and his wife Hannah and her sister Laura.

BIRTHS/BAPTISMS, MARRIAGES, AND DEATH RECORDS

After family records, bibles, diaries, journals, and oral histories have been researched it might be time to pay a visit to the local and or state vital records department. Church records, marriage licenses, marriage logs (check the state national archive and ask to see their marriage logs), cemetery inscriptions, newspaper announcements, wills, school records, military records (which can be requested through the National Archives in Washington, DC), voter records, and the freedman's Bureau Records are all excellent sources when searching births, deaths, and marriages.

SOCIAL SECURITY RECORDS/SOCIAL SECURITY DEATH INDEX (SSDI)

Once you locate someone in the SSDI you can request a copy of their original SS5, the social security application. You can find out parent names, birth place and dates, addresses, and the name of an employer if the person worked at the time of the application. Your research should not only include lines of genealogy but consider simple things such as handwriting, and addresses. I was surprised to learn that my mothers handwriting at the age of 15 matched that of two of my siblings almost exactly. I also learned that my paternal grandfather Charles Bouldin and my maternal grandfather Clarence Washington resided on the same exact block during the same time when they both completed their SS5's, something I never knew.

TAX RECORDS, AND SLAVE ASSESSMENTS

Vital demographic information can be found on both. Slave Assessments are found in the national archives under the owner's name.

COURTS AND REGISTER OF WILLS

In courthouses you can search chancery, land, and probate records. When researching land records look under deeds, sales, mortgages, and manumissions. If researching slaves look under the principal family surname. Also check under "Negroes", during my research I found many slaves who bought their own freedom or that of a family member, in all of these cases they were listed under the surname "Negro". This way of searching is very time consuming because the first and last name of the enslaved only appears once you have begun looking through the documents, however it is worth the time. By searching land records, you can also find copies of mortgages and sales of property. A Will can also provide you with valuable information, like names of surviving relatives, and property owned.

LOCAL HISTORIES

Look for organizations that your family members may joined. Churches, civic organizations, and Unions. If you are researching slaves check Plantation records, and slave advertisements in old newspapers, these can been found in the local Historical Society. Learn everything you can about how when and why slaves were transported to the locale you are researching.

Finally remember to look at every find- two, three, and four times before you determine that it is not important to your research, and even then keep notes and set them someplace where you can access them when you need to look at it again. If at all possible visit the state, or county you are researching, and remember to bring your passion because when you hit a roadblock it will be the only thing that will keep you going.

Afterword

*W*HY ALICE?

The first significant thing that I realized during the early days of my research was Alice's voice. I call this voice her trumpet and in 1862 at the age of seven she blew it for the very first time. By her own account, though a slave she was carefree and innocent as one would suspect a child of that age would be. Her recollection of the event (meeting the President of the United States) which was documented in a 1934 affidavit gives sound to this historical meeting, and allowed Alice to tell it in her own words. Some years later we hear Alice's voice again when she records on the back of a photo of the Bynum Winters Farm that she was the" first colored cook employed by the Winter's from 1889-1903."

Not only has Alice given us insight into her employment status during those years, but she is also making note of the relationship between blacks and whites 25 years after the Emancipation Proclamation.
 In yet another example of Alice's voice, sometime after her father passed away she wrote his birth and death dates at the bottom of his manumission paper, connecting important information that might not have been known about Charles Frazier otherwise.

But more far reaching than writing on documents was Alice declaration that she and her parents were more than just ex-slaves. In later years when Alice was a business woman selling lace and linen from her shop, a Frederick author who had the pleasure of meeting Alice wrote that Alice always greeted visitors to her home with a brief history of who she was, the names of her parents, and where she had come from. The author described Alice Frazier Bouldin as a woman of pride, an unsung hero.

I don't know if Alice Frazier Bouldin was driven by ambition to overcome the overwhelming condition of her people, or if her actions were motivated by her love of family. In either case I believe that she has left us a gift for our senses, the gift of a little girl blowing her trumpet for all to hear.

ABOUT THE AUTHOR

*P*atricia Washington was born in the Bronx, New York the fifth of ten children.

She is employed as an educator for the Hartford Public School District in Connecticut.

She has one daughter, Danielle, an artist.